Surveying Fundamentals for Business Analysts

Surveying Fundamentals for Business Analysts

Carol Deutschlander, CBAP

MANAGEMENTCONCEPTS

MANAGEMENTCONCEPTS
8230 Leesburg Pike, Suite 800
Vienna, VA 22182
(703) 790-9595
Fax: (703) 790-1371
www.managementconcepts.com

Copyright © 2009 by Management Concepts, Inc.

All rights reserved. No part of this book may be reproduced or utilized in any form or by any means, electronic or mechanical, including photocopying, recording, or by an information storage and retrieval system, without permission in writing from the publisher, except for brief quotations in review articles.

Printed in the United States of America

Library of Congress Cataloging-in-Publication Data

Deutschlander, Carol.
    Surveying fundamentals for business analysts / Carol Deutschlander.
      p. cm.
    ISBN 978-1-56726-255-1
1. Business planning. 2. Surveys—Design. 3. Questionnaires—Design. 4. Business analysts. I. Title.
    HD30.28.D479 2009
    001.4'33—dc22
                                                                       2009028703

10   9   8   7   6   5   4   3   2   1

About the Author

Throughout her career, **Carol Deutschlander,** Certified Business Analyst Professional™ (CBAP®), has worked to develop and establish business analysis (BA) best practices and promote the value business analysis brings to projects. She is currently a business analysis manager at Home Hardware Stores Limited, Canada's largest independent home improvement retailer. Prior to joining Home Hardware, Carol was a requirements manager at Research In Motion, a leading designer, manufacturer, and marketer of innovative wireless communications solutions.

Carol's experience includes 19 years in the financial industry. She was an associate director of IT business analysis at MCAP—Canada's largest independent mortgage and equipment financing company—where she coached the company's BA community, developed processes for its system development life cycle, and delivered business requirements and product risk assessments for a variety of projects. Carol was also a business analyst at Sun Life.

Carol is an active supporter of the International Institute of Business Analysis (IIBA®). She has served as a member of the IIBA® Role Delineation and Certification Framework Committees and the IIBA's International Board of Directors. Carol has also served as the IIBA® vice president of education and certification, which allowed her to lead a team of volunteers in the development and launch of the Endorsed Education Provider program and the CBAP® certification program. Her involvement with IIBA® allows her to continue defining the role of the business analyst and to support the CBAP® certification process.

To Carl, for always believing in me.

Contents

Foreword xiii

Preface xv

Introduction: Why Surveys? 1
    Types of Surveys 4
    Surveys and Structured Interviews 4
    The Survey Process 6

Chapter 1: Defining the Objective 7
    Setting Objectives 7
    Determining the Variables and Variations 8

Chapter 2: Identifying the Group 13
    Stakeholders 13
    The Participants 15
        Selecting Potential Participants 16

Chapter 3: Writing Questions 19
    Writing Effective Survey Questions 19
    Types of Questions 20
    Open-Ended Questions 20
        Argument Open-Ended Questions 23
        Single-Response Open-Ended Questions 24

    Closed-Ended Questions 24
        Dichotomous Items 25
        Multiple-Response Items 27
        Interval Scales. 32
        Ranking-Order Scales. 37
        Rating Scales. 41
    Checklist for Writing Good Questions. 44
    Good Habits for Writing Questions 48

Chapter 4: Ordering and Laying Out the Survey 51
    Appearance 51
    The Length of the Survey 53
    The Order of the Questions. 54
    Combining Questions 54

Chapter 5: Piloting the Survey 57
    The Pilot 58
    Selecting the Pilot Participants 59
    The Cover Letter for the Pilot. 59
    Analyzing the Pilot Results. 61

Chapter 6: Sending Out the Survey and Following Up with Participants 63
    The Importance of the Cover Letter 63
    Sending Out the Survey. 66
    Following Up with Participants. 66
    Response Rates 67

Chapter 7: Analyzing and Interpreting the Results 69
    Analyzing Data from Open-Ended Questions 70
    Analyzing Data from Closed-Ended Questions 70
        Frequency Distribution. 71
        Mean. 72
        Median. 74
        Mode. 74
        Range 76

Chapter 8: Reporting on the Results 77
    Possible Audiences for Survey Results 77
    The Written Report 79
    The Presentation 80
    Formatting the Results 83
        Lists 83
        Pie Charts 84
        Bar Charts and Line Charts 85
        Tables 87

Appendix A: Checklist for Writing Good Questions 89

Appendix B: Survey Process Template 91

Appendix C: Question-Writing Template 93

Appendix D: Case Study 95
    Defining the Objectives 96
    Identifying the Stakeholders 99
    Identifying and Selecting Potential Participants 100
    Writing the Survey Questions 101
        Demographic Questions 101
        Questions Related to the First Objective 102
        Questions Related to the Second Objective 104
    Organizing the Survey 110
    The Pilot 110
    Sending Out the Survey 112
    Results: Demographics 113
    Results: The First Objective 118
    Results: The Second Objective 126
    Conclusions 139

Glossary 141

Bibliography 147

Index 149

Foreword

How many times have you wondered about the purpose behind a survey—or about its results and impact? How many surveys have you rushed through with no real regard or thought? Have you wondered how to select an appropriate survey audience? How confident are you that the surveys you create as a business analyst will produce valuable, objective results that contribute to your requirements processes?

If any of these questions are familiar, *Surveying Fundamentals for Business Analysts* is a must-read. Eliciting requirements is an important process needed to make informed business decisions. Only a very small portion of business analysts take the time to use surveys to elicit requirements, and a high percentage of those who do conduct surveys do so with only minimal structure and discipline. *Surveying Fundamentals* guides BAs toward the structure and discipline they need to improve the quality of requirements data.

Carol Deutschlander's comprehensive discussion of the "scientific art" of surveys is impressive. She discusses the various types of surveys, an eight-step approach to the survey process, surveyor objectives, and survey question formats, including question appearance, length, order, and combinations.

Carol also describes how understanding the audience plays an important role in the development and delivery of surveys. She encourages readers to ask essential questions about the survey audience—who, what, where, and why—to uncover the kind of information needed to craft a survey producing maximum results: **Who** will benefit from the survey results? **What** decisions will be made with the output? **Where** will the financial support for this effort come from? **Why** might your audience want to participate in the survey?

Additional material worth highlighting includes a checklist at the end of Chapter 3 with best practices for writing successful questions and a Chapter 5 discussion of the importance of piloting surveys—a verification and validation practice often foregone by BAs who are short on time or resources. Chapter 7 helps readers interpret qualitative and quantitative data objectively, and Chapter 8 clarifies how to present survey results to stakeholders in a variety of formats, including lists, pie charts, bar charts, line charts, and tables. Checklists, templates, and case studies presented in the appendixes provide practical, hands-on best practices.

Readers who don't dog-ear and highlight this important resource will struggle to gather relevant requirements they can trace to organizational goals and objectives. Carefully considering Carol's insightful guidelines will enhance the surveys you create and lead you to more valuable, accurate requirements data.

Glenn R. Brûlé
Executive Director of Client Solutions
ESI International | an Informa business
Vice President of Chapters
International Institute of Business Analysis

Preface

As a business analysis professional, I have consulted many books to find information on using surveys for requirements elicitation, with limited success. Most books devote only a page or two to surveying and do not cover important topics such as how to determine what to include in a survey, when to use each type of question, how to analyze the data collected, and methods of reporting on findings. To effectively conduct a requirements elicitation survey, a business analyst would have to complete independent research on surveying beforehand. Who has that kind of time?

This book offers business analysts detailed information on surveying. As you work through the chapters, you will find general information about surveys and learn about the different types of surveys and the process of completing a survey. The book explains how to identify your stakeholders and participants, how to write different types of effective questions, and how to use each kind of question in a survey. It also offers practical examples of questions. In addition, the book explains how to lay out a survey, conduct a pilot, send out the survey, conduct follow-up, analyze the data, and report your findings. At the end of the book, there is a comprehensive case study that walks you through the entire survey development and administration process.

This book gives enough basic information to boost your confidence in your ability to create and administer surveys. It will also be a reference for subsequent survey efforts. I hope you enjoy this book and learn as much reading it as I learned writing it. Keep up the good work!

Carol Deutschlander
Waterloo, Ontario

INTRODUCTION

Why Surveys?

The International Institute of Business Analysis (IIBA®) defines *surveying* as "a means of eliciting information from many people, anonymously, in a relatively short time" (IIBA® 2006, 177). Surveys are also called *questionnaires*. In the IIBA® *Business Analysis Body of Knowledge®* (*BABOK®*), the terms *questionnaire* and *survey* are used interchangeably. We will do the same throughout this book.

In the nineteenth century, Sir Francis Galton invented the questionnaire for use by psychologists (Rathus 2004, 23). Surveying, therefore, is not a new technique, but surveys are used less often in projects than are other elicitation techniques. A recent study conducted by the IIBA® indicated that 28 percent of all participants do not use surveying as an elicitation technique, 50 percent occasionally use the technique, and only 22 percent of participants regularly use surveying to elicit requirements (Figure I-1).[1]

When business analysts use surveying to elicit requirements, they examine and interpret the results, which become a source of requirements. Surveying can be used as the sole elicitation technique, but more often it is used in addition to other elicitation techniques. A survey may focus on the participant's opinions or on factual information, depending on its objective. For business analysts, surveys can be used:

- To understand users' reactions to an existing product
- To determine the relative priority of product features

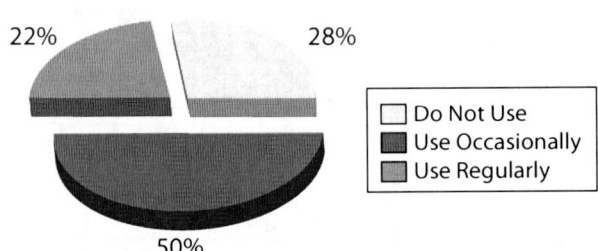

FIGURE I-1: Use of Surveying as an Elicitation Technique

Source: IIBA® BABOK® Techniques Survey, 2008

- To identify an existing solution's strengths and weaknesses
- To identify potential scope items
- As input to other requirements elicitation activities
- To identify changes users would like made to an existing system
- To gather feedback from a requirements workshop that can be used to improve future workshops
- To gather feedback from potential vendors of commercial off-the-shelf (COTS) packages as part of a request for information (RFI) or request for proposal (RFP) process.

Surveying can be used in addition to other elicitation techniques. For example:

- Interview results on a specific topic could be used as input to survey questions.
- Results from a survey question might be used to elicit greater detail in interviews.
- A small subset of requirements could be explored using a survey, while other sets of requirements may be elicited through workshops or interviews.

INTRODUCTION Why Surveys?

The advantages of using surveys include:

- Flexibility to ask almost anything.
- The ability to gather information from a large group of people.
- The possibility of anonymity for participants.
- Gaining access to users who are not able to participate in interviews. Some users might not be able to participate in interviews because they lack the time to commit to an interview or live in a different time zone. There could also be too many people to get input from, which would require you to interview some and survey the rest.
- Simplicity of administration.
- Simplicity of analysis and compilation of results.
- Uniformity. All participants are asked the same questions, ensuring the consistency of data collection.
- The ability to sample a population instead of requiring universal participation. The business analyst can make reasonable extrapolations from the sample to the entire population.

Using surveys also has several disadvantages:

- Surveying is not always a substitute for interviewing. Qualitative data is hard to obtain in surveys.
- Surveys do not provide an opportunity to ask participants follow-up questions about their responses. This is especially problematic if participants' responses are unclear.
- Participants may misinterpret questions because they cannot ask for clarification.
- Surveys garner lower response rates than do other methods of gathering information, such as interviews.

Consider these advantages and disadvantages carefully before deciding whether it is appropriate to include a survey in the elicitation plan for your project.

Types of Surveys

There are three types of surveys: self-administered, group-administered, and mail-out.

- **Self-administered:** The business analyst conducting the survey meets with each participant to explain the purpose of the survey, and then the participant completes the survey independently. The business analyst may or may not be present while the participant answers the survey. This is often a matter of preference that can be discussed with the participant.

- **Group-administered:** A group of participants completes the survey at the same time under supervision so that discussion among participants is controlled. The business analyst answers participants' questions. Group-administered surveys can be more effective to administer. This type of survey allows participants to ask for clarification on questions. You can be fairly confident that you will obtain a higher response rate.

- **Mail-out:** The survey is sent to the participant, and the participant and the business analyst have no contact. Mail-out surveys can be sent as hard copies or in email, or they can be web-based. They are very useful if you have a limited budget, your questions are very straightforward, or you need to gather input from a large group of participants. Mail-out surveys do not allow the business analyst to ask participants for additional information, so strong, well-written questions are the key to ensuring valuable results.

Surveys and Structured Interviews

Surveys and structured interviews are very similar; both techniques require that questions be defined ahead of time. The advantage of interviews is that they allow the business analyst to ask participants additional questions about their responses.

When conducting an interview, either in person or over the phone, ensure that participants do not feel threatened by how the information might be

INTRODUCTION Why Surveys?

used. Whenever possible, be honest with participants about how the outcome may affect an individual or group. Before beginning an interview, decide what you will say if a participant asks about potential fallout or consequences. You may have to contact a manager, a project sponsor, or a member of a communications team for advice.

If we expand the definition of *survey* to include interviews, there are three more methods of administering surveys: by telephone, one on one, and in a focus group.

- **Telephone:** A telephone survey should be no more than 15 minutes in length. Each participant must be presented with exactly the same questions in the same order because participants may answer questions differently depending on the preceding questions. The survey can include any combination of open-ended or closed-ended questions (see Chapter 3 for more on question types).

- **One-on-one:** These surveys can be longer than telephone surveys, often requiring an hour or more to complete. The business analyst meets with the participant and asks the participant each question on the survey. As in a telephone survey, each participant must be presented with exactly the same well-defined questions in the same order. The business analyst may deviate from the plan as needed to further explore a participant's responses.

- **Focus groups:** Focus groups are composed of prequalified individuals who share their opinions, needs, or impressions in an interactive group setting. A business analyst facilitates the discussion. Focus groups are widely used in marketing to elicit requirements or feedback. They can be used in the surveying process to elicit or verify usability requirements or to pilot the survey.

When management is planning to make important business decisions based on the data gleaned from a survey, the business analyst should follow up with interviews to verify the survey data. For instance, usability studies generally start with a survey and are followed by focus groups.

The Survey Process

Conducting surveys is an eight-step process:

1. Defining the objective
2. Identifying the group to be surveyed
3. Writing questions
4. Ordering and laying out the survey
5. Piloting the survey
6. Sending out the survey and following up with participants
7. Analyzing and interpreting the results
8. Reporting on the results.

Subsequent chapters will discuss each step in detail.

When planning a survey, consider:

- How much time and what resources will be necessary to complete all survey development activities
- The deadline for completing the analysis
- The processes needed to collect data, contact participants, produce the survey, conduct the analysis, and produce the results report
- Whether external specialists will be required throughout the survey process
- How you will gain the approval required to conduct the survey and to contact members of the target audience
- What data analysis method will yield results that facilitate decision-making.

Note

1. International Institute of Business Analysis, Survey Techniques in BABOK® v2, November 7, 2008. For more information, see http://blog.theiiba.org/2008/11/techniques-in-babok-v2.html.

CHAPTER 1
Defining the Objective

Before you can begin writing effective survey questions, you must understand what the survey is trying to accomplish. This can be done by identifying the objective or objectives of the survey. These objectives are broken down into possible variables and variations and further analyzed. This information is then used to write the survey questions. The objectives will be the guide to creating an effective survey and effective questions. You should be able to trace each question in the survey back to a single objective.

Setting Objectives

The objective of the survey may be taken directly from project documentation, such as the business case or problem definition. But if the survey is one of many elicitation activities, you may have to put more effort into determining the objectives for the survey in particular. When setting objectives for the survey, ask:

- What is the overall goal of the survey?
- What question(s) must be answered?
- What will be done with the data collected?
- What decisions could be affected based on the information collected?
- How will data be reported, and who will see the results?

- How can we determine whether the right information has been collected?
- Who will act on the data?

Start with one or more general objectives, and refine them as you go along. For example, if the general objective is to evaluate the new system that product specialists have recently begun using, related specific objectives might include:

- Understanding how the system is being used
- Determining user satisfaction with the new system
- Identifying changes that have resulted from implementing the new system.

Each concept or idea should be stated as a single objective. If the word "and" is used when stating an objective, it probably consists of two objectives. The more focused and clear the objectives are, the more likely the survey will gather the information needed.

Determining the Variables and Variations

Next, for each single objective, identify the specific information that must be collected. Determine the variables for each objective. Let's say we are looking at satisfaction with the new system. For each variable identified, such as overall satisfaction, dig deeper. Can overall satisfaction be assessed, and then broken down into specific components, such as satisfaction with available data, system response time, and the usefulness of data? Ask what other variables might help explain why some users are satisfied and others are dissatisfied with the system.

The challenge is to think of all possible variables that may help collect the correct information. For example, user satisfaction may be affected by the training users received. Was it enough training? Was the training in the right format? What do the users think about their jobs? How does the system help them do their jobs? Does the new system make tasks easier than they used to be? Each variable and its components or variations will be used to develop questions.

Some variations may require further analysis and breaking down. For example, if the survey is looking at how users view their jobs now that the new system has been implemented, for the variation "view their jobs," consider asking questions that address:

- How much users valued the interaction they had with other departments before the system was implemented.
- How concerned users are about maintaining existing relationships with other departments. In other words, if the system will conduct transactions that previously were carried out through conversations among departments, this might result in less interaction among the departments.
- Whether they feel the system has increased the professionalism of their jobs. If the users were previously in a paper-based manual environment (outdated) and now are operating in an environment with technology, do they feel more professional?

This analysis and breakdown can lead to more questions. For example, you might ask whether the new features being proposed for the new system would enhance or constrain interdepartmental interaction and relationships and professionalism.

Mind mapping tools (Figure 1-1) are a great way to quickly trace your objective to its variables and variations.

Once all variables and variations for each objective have been identified, determine which ones will be used to write questions. Depending on the length of the survey, all or only some variables and variations may be used. This process of breaking down objectives into smaller variables and variations on which all questions are based allows each question to be traced back to a single objective.

Once all objectives have been finalized, look at each objective and identify the target audience for questions about that objective. You may ask all

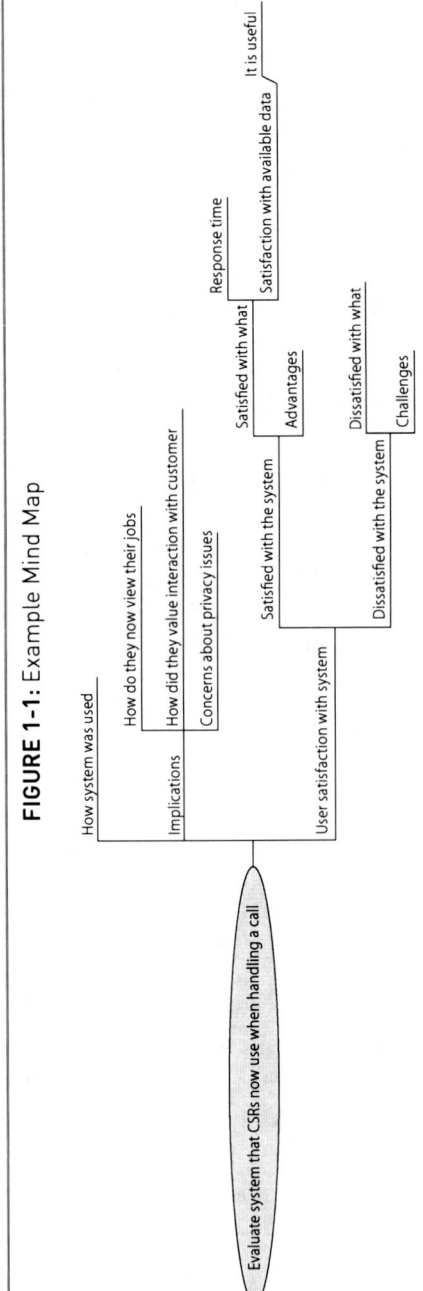

FIGURE 1-1: Example Mind Map

the participants about all the objectives or present subsets of questions to different segments of participants.

Depending on the type and size of the initiative, additional preparation may be warranted before proceeding with the survey. This additional work could include identifying participants, interviewing or having informal discussions with participants, analyzing relevant literature (in trade magazines, for example), or researching similar product features on the Internet.

CHAPTER 2
Identifying the Group

In any initiative a business analyst undertakes, it is important to know who the stakeholders are. Once they have been identified, some stakeholders are further categorized as potential participants. This chapter will help you identify stakeholders. It also offers methods to identify your potential participants and determine participant requirements.

Stakeholders

Identifying the right people to participate in a survey is important. When preparing for a survey, completing a stakeholder analysis can help. The following questions can help you determine who the stakeholders for the survey are:

- Who needs the information that will be gathered from the survey?
- Who will make decisions using the results of the survey?
- Who else would be interested in the results?
- Whose area of work may be affected by the outcome of the survey?
- Who is paying for the survey?
- Will anyone be uncomfortable with the survey?
- Who must participate in survey planning?

- Whose permission is required before potential participants are contacted?
- Whose support is critical to making the survey successful?
- Who might participate in the actual survey?

Once you have identified the stakeholders, plan how best to engage each group in the survey process. For instance, stakeholders identified as key participants in the planning of the survey may need more information, such as background details (e.g., survey objectives potential, survey participants, why the survey is being conducted, how the results will be used). A survey participant may need to receive only the cover letter and the actual survey.

Some stakeholders may be engaged throughout the survey development process. When working with stakeholders, remember that:[1]

- The stakeholders who specify the objectives often will not agree on the objectives.
- The stakeholders themselves may be uncertain about the objectives because of their differing experiences and perspectives.
- One stakeholder may say, "We don't need to ask that question. We already know the answer"; other stakeholders may disagree because they themselves do not know the answer.
- Scope creep is very common. Stakeholders may try to cover everything they want to know in a single survey. It can be very difficult to get them to think clearly, focus the objectives, and avoid turning a 20-item survey into a 100-item survey. They may say, "Since we're sending this survey out anyway, why not add just one more question on this topic?"

A simple stakeholder analysis chart (Figure 2-1) can be used to organize your stakeholders and understand their needs.

CHAPTER 2 Identifying the Group   **15**

FIGURE 2-1: Example Stakeholder Analysis Chart

Stakeholder Name	Stakeholder Category (e.g., decision maker, executive, participant, project sponsor, project team member)	Interest in Survey (i.e., Why is the stakeholder involved? What does the stakeholder want to get out of the survey? How will the stakeholder be impacted by results?)	What the Stakeholder is Expected to Provide

The Participants

The *potential participants*—people invited to participate in the survey—are an important subgroup of stakeholders.

How are potential participants selected? To select the most appropriate participants, clear objectives for the survey should already be established. For example, if the purpose of a survey is to identify scope items for system enhancements, it may be appropriate to select a wide variety of participants, including senior leaders, business managers, and system users. If the survey results will be used to prioritize features, decision makers may be the only participants.

Depending on the objective of the survey, segmenting the participants and asking each segment different questions may work well. For example, if the survey is being conducted to identify enhancements to a user interface, participants may be segmented into daily users, occasional users, power users, and new users.

If the population of potential participants is small (i.e., 150 or less), consider including the entire group in the survey. However, if the group is larger, numbering in the thousands, select a portion of the population to include in the survey. This group is called a *sample*. The sample selected from the population should be representative of the entire group. The results from this portion of the group will be similar to what would be learned if the entire group were included in the survey.

There may be situations in which the business analyst chooses to *oversample*—overrepresent—a portion of the population. This is appropriate if a survey's purpose is to draw conclusions about one or more subgroups within the population. Some national surveys oversample minorities to ensure that there are enough minority respondents to draw reliable conclusions. In a business setting, a business analyst may want to oversample small departments for the same reason.

If the results of the survey will be used to make an important or key business decision, survey as large a group as possible to ensure accuracy and full representation. If the decision is less important, using a smaller group will save time and money.

Selecting Potential Participants

Several methods can be used when selecting potential participants.

- **Systematic (random) sampling:** Every nth name is selected from a list of potential participants. First, list members of the population in an Excel spreadsheet. Excel's Random function can be used to assign a random number to each member of the population. Sort the members according to random number, then select the number of participants required for the survey. Every member of the population has an equal chance of being selected. This is the most accurate approach to sampling.

- **Convenience sampling:** Participants are selected based on how convenient it is to contact them. For example, all staff in a given location may be chosen as participants. This method is less accurate, but it can provide useful information if all key characteristics of the population are represented in the sample. This method may also increase the response rate.

- **Snowball sampling:** A few participants are contacted and asked to refer other potential participants. This method is useful when an extensive contact list is not available, but it is less accurate than systematic or convenience sampling.

- **Recruited sampling:** The participants are recruited by phone, email, or in person. Using this method may create a representative sample, depending on how participants are selected. To ensure you have a random sample, use a multi-method approach such as contacting participants by phone and then asking them to log on to a website to complete the survey. If the initial selection is random (i.e., all people in the population have an equal chance of being selected), the second step of completing a survey online will maintain the integrity of the selection as long as all selected participants have equal access to the website.

- **Unrestricted sampling:** Participants include anyone who finds and takes the survey (for example, on the Internet). This is the least accurate sampling method.

Consider these factors when selecting potential participants:

- Is there a chance that some potential participants will not take the survey seriously or give the questions full thought?

- Is there a chance that someone else will complete the survey instead of the potential participant? Provide good information upfront about why the survey is being conducted and how the information will be used. You can also ensure the confidentiality of the responses.

- Will potential participants want to remain anonymous?

- Could the group of potential participants be excessively biased? Sometimes the sponsor will have particular people in mind to participate who may not provide the most constructive feedback. If this is a possibility, be proactive—provide a list of suggested potential respondents for approval to your project sponsor.

These factors can lead to less valid data if you do not consider them ahead of time and build in measures to counter their effects.

In some organizations, potential participants may be identified not by the business analyst but by the executive sponsor or other business leader on the project. They will have specific reasons for identifying particular participants. These suggested participants must be included in the group, but you should review the final survey distribution list to ensure that participants are unbiased and offer a perspective that represents the opinion of the majority.

Note

1. This list was provided by Dr. Shelley Kirkpatrick, Director of Assessment Services at Management Concepts, and is based on her personal experiences.

CHAPTER 3

Writing Questions

Once you know the objectives of your survey and who will be asked to participate, the fun begins. This chapter will walk you through different types of survey questions and the advantages and disadvantages of each type of question. It provides practical examples, suggests situations in which each type of question can be used, and offers guidelines for writing each type of question and effective questions in general.

Writing Effective Survey Questions

The business analyst can start to write the survey questions using the objectives, variables, and variations identified as input. Each question included in the survey should have a purpose. Before adding a question to a survey, the business analyst must understand how information from the question will be used.

For each survey question:

- Write a draft question.
- Try different forms of the same question.
- Revise and rewrite the question as needed (e.g., after getting feedback from the pilot group).
- Confirm, after each change, that the question will provide the information needed.

Types of Questions

Survey questions address four different aspects of human thought and behavior.

1. *What people say they want; their attitudes.* Questions about attitudes are useful when gathering input on functionality, developing a wish list, determining scope, or developing potential business rules.

2. *What people think is true; their beliefs.* Questions about beliefs will help you gather opinions. You might ask, "Is the system reliable?" or "Do you think doing X will solve Y?"

3. *What people do; their behavior.* Questions about behavior can be useful when looking at the usability of a system. For example, you might ask, "Do you use hot keys?"

4. *What people are; their attributes.* Questions about attributes can be used to gather information about the participants themselves. Examples include "What is your role?" if you want to identify the participant's level of accountability, or "How many years have you been in this role?" if you want to determine whether the user is new or experienced.

Depending on the objectives of the survey, you may use all or just one type of question. For each type of question, you may choose one or more question formats. Let's look at the different question formats used in surveys.

Open-Ended Questions

Open-ended questions allow for a wide range of responses. They are generally not answered with a simple one-word response. Participants answer these questions in their own words; they are not given a list of possible answers.

Open-ended questions have many benefits:

- They work well if you do not know what kinds of responses the questions will generate.
- They stimulate free thought.
- The answers are relatively uninfluenced by the business analyst.
- They encourage participants to draw upon their memories.
- They allow the business analyst to learn the language the participants use (for subsequent work).
- They help the business analyst identify what information or misinformation participants have.
- They are ideal if there are many possible answers to a question, such as "What is your occupation?"

Open-ended questions also have a number of disadvantages:

- It may be difficult to manage the wide variety of responses. Each participant may answer each question differently.
- It is time-consuming to analyze the results and interpret the data.
- The participants must recall and organize ideas when answering questions, which can be challenging.
- Answers may be vague, requiring additional clarification.
- It is difficult to know whether responses contain errors or omissions.
- Answering the questions requires more effort than answering closed-ended questions.
- Participants may be afraid to put ideas or opinions in writing.
- Participants usually know more than their answers suggest.
- Participants' answers may not provide the information the business analyst needs.

Here are some sample open-ended questions.

- What do you like most about . . . ?

- What do you like least about . . . ?
- Tell me how you feel about. . . .
- What does X mean to you?
- What current government regulations apply to the management of inventory?
- How much is the retail sales division expected to grow in the next three years?
- What types of user disabilities must the system account for?
- What modifications do you think should be included in the next release?
- What browser versions must be supported when we implement the new customer website?
- What unusual environmental conditions must the design of the new warehouse address?

Open-ended questions are useful when you would like to:

- Determine which participants know what about an area of interest.
- Identify the most common types of misinformation participants have.
- Figure out what pieces of information are most widely known.
- Determine what types of information participants lack.
- Understand opinions.
- Explore an area of interest, then use the results from open-ended questions to develop closed-ended questions for a subsequent survey with a different sample group.
- Determine what is important to people; participants tend to mention what is most essential.
- Make sure a survey with closed-ended questions has addressed all important points. An open-ended question at the end of a closed-

ended survey could ask if there is anything else the participant would like to add that hasn't been adequately addressed.

When using open-ended questions, don't use too many in a single questionnaire. Use two or three at most, or participants may give up on completing the survey. They are best used with a smaller group of participants.

If most participants reply "other" to a closed-ended question, an open-ended question probably should have been used instead. If you are interviewing additional people, you could use an open-ended question instead to investigate the subject further. You would not redo the survey, but it could serve as a lesson learned for next time.

There are two kinds of open-ended questions: argument open-ended questions and single-response open-ended questions.

Argument Open-Ended Questions

Argument questions ask the participant about both sides of an issue. Examples include "What are the advantages of X?" "What are the disadvantages of X?" These paired questions help prevent biased results because they look at both sides of an issue.

More examples of argument open-ended questions include:

- What are the advantages of the current audit process? What are the disadvantages of the current audit process?
- In what ways does the current process documentation meet your needs? In what ways does the current process documentation not meet your needs?
- Which parts of the Sarbanes-Oxley Act are the easiest to integrate into your business processes? Which parts of the Sarbanes-Oxley Act are the most difficult to integrate into your business processes?
- When would be the worst time during the week to bring the system down for maintenance? When would be the best time during the week to bring the system down for maintenance?

- Which parts of the system do you find easiest to use? Which parts of the system do you find most difficult to use?

Single-Response Open-Ended Questions

Single-response questions are intended to elicit a brief, factual answer. Examples include:

- What year were you born?
- What was your total income last year?
- What is your job title?
- What is the maximum acceptable down time for the system?
- What is the current volume of deposit transactions per month?
- What is the expected volume of deposit transactions per month in 2010?
- How many customer records currently exist?
- How many customer records are expected to exist in 2010?
- How many users must access the system at the same time?
- How long do system access logs need to be kept?

There is risk associated with single-response questions: If a participant does not know the exact answers, he or she may guess, yielding inaccurate information. Some participants may not answer certain questions, especially those pertaining to personal information like their age. These participants might be willing to answer the same questions if they are able to choose an answer in a range. Questions with answers in range format will be discussed later in this chapter.

Closed-Ended Questions

Closed-ended questions offer the participant a list of options to select from. This kind of question has several benefits:

- Closed-ended questions are easy for the participant to answer.
- Results can be analyzed more quickly and easily.
- Closed-ended questions allow you to cover a lot of ground in a single survey. You can ask more closed-ended questions than you can open-ended questions.
- The response choices may clarify the questions.

Closed-ended questions also have a few disadvantages:

- The most accurate answer (from a participant's perspective) may not be provided, but the participant may answer the question anyway. The results may then be inaccurate.
- The limited response options provided may limit the usefulness and the amount of data collected.
- The response options imply the type of response desired.

This chapter will explore five specific types of closed-ended questions:

- Dichotomous items
- Multiple-response items
- Interval scales
- Ranking-order scales
- Rating-scales.

Dichotomous Items

Dichotomous items are nominal closed-ended questions. They do not measure amounts. Instead, they are typically used to gather factual information. Dichotomous items allow the participant to select one of two possible responses. If neither answer choice for a particular question is applicable, the participant may choose not answer the question.

Examples of dichotomous items include:

- Have you used surveying as an elicitation technique?
  Yes ___ No ___
- Is the solution required to use organizational web standards?
  Yes ___ No ___
- Is the solution required to use organizational brand standards?
  Yes ___ No ___
- Is the system business-critical? Yes ___ No ___
- How many times have you used the online help manual in the past three weeks?
  More than ten times _____ Ten or less times _____
- Are the updates to customer data required in real time ____ or overnight ____?
- Is remote user access required for this system? Yes ___ No ___

Dichotomous items have two benefits. They are simple for participants to answer because only two answer choices are provided. They also simplify compiling results. However, dichotomous items leave out the possible range of answers between the two choices provided, so they may lead to the collection of erroneous data.[1] Also, they don't allow participants to elaborate on their answers or add relevant information.

This type of question may be useful when:

- You are verifying the type of participant. For example, if the sample is segmented into management and non-management, the survey may include a question asking the participant in which category he or she belongs. Results from this question would be used during data analysis to determine whether there are differences in responses between the two segments.
- The survey is about a requirement with only two possible options.
- You are determining which of two possible decisions or outcomes users prefer.

CHAPTER 3 Writing Questions   **27**

Dichotomous item questions are fairly easy to write. The response categories must include all possible responses. You might include "uncertain" as a response choice along with "yes" and "no" to ensure the response categories are exhaustive. If a third option is provided, however, the question is no longer a dichotomous item, but a multiple-response closed-ended question.

Multiple-Response Items

Multiple-response items are another type of nominal closed-ended question. They allow the participant to select one or more options from a list. Multiple-response items may also be called multiple-choice questions, categorical response items, or checklists. The options in a multiple-response item list do not have a logical order or a relationship with the other options in the list.

A *partially closed-ended question* is a specific type of multiple-response question. Partially closed-ended questions offer a compromise. They allow the participant to pick one of the answers provided or answer "other," and space is provided for the participant to write in an alternative response. Note that offering an "other" response choice rarely yields much additional information from participants.

Examples of multiple-response item questions include:

- If you have used surveys before, what was their purpose? Please select all that apply.

    a) ___ Prioritizing requirements

    b) ___ Identifying the strengths and weaknesses of an existing solution

    c) ___ Understanding user satisfaction with an existing solution

    d) ___ Gathering input for other requirements elicitation activities

    e) ___ Identifying potential scope items

    f) ___ Obtaining input on functionality

g) ___ Gathering facts

h) ___ Identifying changes users would like to make to an existing system

i) ___ Other; please specify _____

- What would you like to learn about before conducting a survey? Please check all that apply.

    a) ___ The overall survey process

    b) ___ How to lay out or design a survey

    c) ___ How to write effective survey questions

    d) ___ Types of questions to use

    e) ___ Types of questions to avoid

    f) ___ Sample questions

    g) ___ How to analyze data

    h) ___ How to interpret survey results

    i) ___ How to apply survey results

    j) ___ Tools available to administer surveys

    k) ___ Other; please specify_____

- How often are updates to data required?

    a) ___ In real time

    b) ___ Near real time (within two seconds)

    c) ___ Overnight

- What languages must the solution support? Please select all that apply.

    a) ___ English

    b) ___ French

CHAPTER 3 Writing Questions

    c) ___ Spanish

    d) ___ Mandarin

    e) ___ German

    f) ___ Italian

    g) ___ Other; please specify _____

- Which North American locations will be using this solution? Please select all that apply.

    a) ___ Toronto, Ontario

    b) ___ Vancouver, British Columbia

    c) ___ New York, New York

    d) ___ Austin, Texas

    e) ___ Seattle, Washington

    f) ___ Miami, Florida

- What browser versions must be supported when we implement the new customer website? Please select all that apply.

    a) ___ Internet Explorer version 5.0 and up

    b) ___ Netscape version 6.0 and up

    c) ___ Firefox version 3.0 and up

    d) ___ Safari version 4.0 and up

    e) ___ Opera version 4.0 and up

- Which of the following groups will use the system? Please select all that apply.

    a) ___ Accounting clerks

    b) ___ Cashiers

    c) ___ Store managers

- d) ___ Customers
- e) ___ IT support teams
- f) ___ Other; please specify _____

- Which of the following features will users of the system require? Please select all that apply.
  - a) ___ Online screen-level help
  - b) ___ Online field-level help
  - c) ___ Hot key functionality
  - d) ___ Field-level warning messages
  - e) ___ Field-level error messages
  - f) ___ Other; please specify _____

- Who should have access to audit information? Please select all that apply.
  - a) ___ Financial analysts
  - b) ___ IT auditor
  - c) ___ Senior management
  - d) ___ External auditors
  - e) ___ Compliance officer
  - f) ___ Other; please specify _____

- What type of access will external auditors need to audit information?
  - a) ___ Read-only
  - b) ___ Read and update
  - c) ___ Add, read, and update
  - d) ___ Add, read, update, and delete

CHAPTER 3 Writing Questions

- How often must the system be backed up?
    a) ___ Hourly
    b) ___ Twice per calendar day
    c) ___ Daily
    d) ___ Weekly
    e) ___ Monthly
- What regulations apply to the solution? Please select all that apply.
    a) ___ Sarbanes-Oxley legislation
    b) ___ Americans with Disabilities Act (ADA)
    c) ___ State employment standards
    d) ___ Regional labor laws
    e) ___ Transportation of dangerous goods regulations
    f) ___ Other; please specify _____

Multiple-response items have several advantages:

- They allow the participant to select one or more answers.
- It is easy to analyze the results.
- They are easy to answer.
- Participants are more likely to answer them than they are to answer open-ended questions.

This type of question also has a few disadvantages:

- Including "other" as a response option usually does not glean much additional information.
- When many response options are provided, participants may become confused or lose interest.
- Data gathered will be inaccurate if you do not provide all possible response options.

Consider using multiple-response item questions when:

- Determining the features a user would want included in a release.
- A requirement must be clarified, and the possible options are already known (for example, "Who needs access to this system?" or "What type of access does this user need?").
- Determining what kind of support is required (for example, which web browsers must be supported), and known constraints exist (for example, IT will support only a certain number of options).

When constructing multiple-response item questions, remember to follow these important rules:

- The response categories must include all possible responses. Use "uncertain" or "other" along with "yes" and "no" to ensure the response categories are exhaustive.
- The response categories cannot overlap. Each option in the list must be mutually exclusive. For example, "hockey" and "team sports" should not be response options for the same question.
- Each response option must contain a single idea.
- An option of "types of questions to use *and* avoid" is not correct. The options provided should be two separate questions:
    - Types of question to use
    - Types of questions to avoid

Interval Scales

Interval closed-ended questions have a logical order, and there is an equal difference between adjacent categories. Here's a sample question:

What are your monthly costs?

a) ___ Under $99.99

b) ___ $100.00 to $199.99

CHAPTER 3 Writing Questions

  c) ___ $200.00 to $299.99

  d) ___ $300.00 to $399.99

  e) ___ $400.00 or more

Interval questions are used to gather quantitative information, such as years of service, income, and age.

Other examples of interval questions include:

- How many users will need to access the system at the same time?

  a) ___ Less than 100

  b) ___ 101 to 200

  c) ___ 201 to 300

  d) ___ More than 301

- How many users will need to access the system when it is implemented?

  a) ___ Less than 100

  b) ___ 101 to 200

  c) ___ 201 to 300

  d) ___ 301 to 400

  e) ___ 401 to 500

  f) ___ More than 501

- How many users will need to access the system in 2010?

  a) ___ Less than 100

  b) ___ 101 to 200

  c) ___ 201 to 300

  d) ___ 301 to 400

  e) ___ 401 to 500

  f) ___ More than 501

- How much system downtime is acceptable in a 24-hour period?
  a) ___ Less than 5 minutes
  b) ___ 6 minutes to 30 minutes
  c) ___ 31 minutes to 1 hour
  d) ___ More than 1 hour[2]
- Which of the following is the *best* time for a system to be unavailable?
  a) ___ Midnight to 3:00 a.m.
  b) ___ 3:01 a.m. to 6:00 a.m.
  c) ___ 6:01 a.m. to 9:00 a.m.
  d) ___ 9:01 a.m. to noon
  e) ___ 12:01 p.m. to 3:00 p.m.
  f) ___ 3:01 p.m. to 6:00 p.m.
  g) ___ 6:01 p.m. to 9:00 p.m.
  h) ___ 9:01 p.m. to 11:59 p.m.
- Which is the *worst* possible time for a system to be unavailable?
  a) ___ Midnight to 3:00 a.m.
  b) ___ 3:01 a.m. to 6:00 a.m.
  c) ___ 6:01 a.m. to 9:00 a.m.
  d) ___ 9:01 a.m. to noon
  e) ___ 12:01 p.m. to 3:00 p.m.
  f) ___ 3:01 p.m. to 6:00 p.m.
  g) ___ 6:01 p.m. to 9:00 p.m.
  h) ___ 9:01 p.m. to 11:59 p.m.

CHAPTER 3 Writing Questions

- When moving from one screen to the next within the system, what is the required response time?
    a) ___ Less than one second
    b) ___ Two seconds to three seconds
    c) ___ Four seconds to five seconds
    d) ___ More than five seconds
- How many customer records currently exist?
    a) ___ 1,000 to 4,999
    b) ___ 5,000 to 9,999
    c) ___ 10,000 to 14,999
    d) ___ More than 15,000
- How many customer records are expected to exist in 2010?
    a) ___ 1,000 to 4,999
    b) ___ 5,000 to 9,999
    c) ___ 10,000 to 14,999
    d) ___ More than 15,000
- Historical inventory information must be retained for:
    a) ___ The current month plus the previous calendar month
    b) ___ The current month plus the previous two calendar months
    c) ___ The current month plus the previous three calendar months
    d) ___ The current month plus the previous four calendar months
    e) ___ The current month plus the previous five calendar months
- If a disaster was declared, when would you need the system restored?
    a) ___ Within one hour
    b) ___ Within two hours

- c) ___ Within three hours
- d) ___ After more than three hours

■ If your system must be restored with data from a backup, how recent must the data be?

- a) ___ Within one hour from failure
- b) ___ Within two hours from failure
- c) ___ Within three hours from failure
- d) ___ Within four hours from failure
- e) ___ From the previous business day

■ How long have you used the current system?

- a) ___ Less than one year
- b) ___ One year to five years
- c) ___ Six years to ten years
- d) ___ More than ten years

Interval scale questions:

- ■ Are useful when only one answer in the range must be selected
- ■ Are useful if results will be presented in a graphical format (for example, if responses will be plotted across a range)
- ■ Are good for comparative work
- ■ Are appropriate when data within ranges are adequate for analysis
- ■ Simplify data analysis.

Interval scale questions also have a couple of disadvantages:

- ■ Data analysis cannot show whether there is a significant difference within a range. For example, in a one- to nine-minute interval, the eight-minute mark might be significant to participants, but the data will not show that.

CHAPTER 3 Writing Questions   **37**

- The most appropriate answer may be outside the ranges provided.

This type of question is useful when gathering quantitative data such as:

- Current number of users and expected growth
- Current number of transactions per frequency and expected growth
- Current number of types of records and expected growth
- Nonfunctional requirements for retention
- Nonfunctional requirements for system availability
- Nonfunctional requirements for performance.

When constructing interval closed-ended questions, follow these important rules:

- Intervals should be equal; for example, each response option should increase by 9 or 99.
- Make sure there are no overlapping categories. For example, do not state numerical ranges of 10 to 20 and 20 to 30. The ranges should instead be written as 10 to 19, 20 to 29, and 30 to 39.
- List categories in logical order (1–10, 11–20, and 21–30, not 1–10, 21–30, and 11–20).
- The categories must be mutually exclusive.

Ranking-Order Scales

A *ranking-order scale item* is a type of ordinal closed-ended question. *Ordinal closed-ended questions* allow the participant to place options in an ordered sequence. For example, the participant may be asked to prioritize possible scope items ("Please rank the top three features you would like to see in the next release."). The participant should not be asked to rank more than ten options.

A ranking-order scale question may also use paired comparisons, in which the participant is given two options and is asked to choose between them. As a general rule, do not use more than 15 comparisons in one survey.

Ranking-order scale questions are used to gather factual information but can also be used to gather opinions, attitudes, or judgments. A survey may combine types of questions. For example, it might start with a ranking-order question on priorities that is followed up with a rating-scale question to validate the previous answer.

Sample ranking-order closed-ended questions include:

- I prefer ___ radial buttons ___ checkboxes.
- Between system response time of less than two seconds from screen to screen and 99 percent system availability in a 24-hour period, I prefer ___ system response time ___ system availability.
- Between Arial font and Verdana font, I choose ___ Arial ___ Verdana.
- Are you in favor of ___ or against ___ changing the screen background to white?
- Do you expect system performance to be equal to ___ or better than ___ its current performance?
- Please rank the top three items you would like to be included in the next release.

    a) ___ Online screen-level help
    b) ___ Online field-level help
    c) ___ Field-level warning messages
    d) ___ Field-level error messages
    e) ___ Screen-level warning messages
    f) ___ Screen-level error messages

CHAPTER 3 Writing Questions   **39**

- Please rank the following items in order of importance from 1 to 5, where 1 is most important.

    a) ___ Audit reports

    b) ___ Retention of financial transaction information

    c) ___ Protecting the privacy of customer information

    d) ___ Controlled access to the system

    e) ___ Ability to restore the system within one hour

- Please identify your top three priorities from 1 to 3, with 1 being your top priority.

    a) ___ Adhering to privacy regulations

    b) ___ Complying with Sarbanes-Oxley legislation

    c) ___ Meeting Americans with Disabilities Act requirements

    d) ___ Ensuring corporate branding standards are met

    e) ___ Following corporate security policy

- The following issues have been identified as important ones to fix in the next release. Please rank the three issues you believe are most important from 1 to 3, with 1 being the most important.

    a) ___ Immediate access to historical data from the past three calendar months

    b) ___ Improved response time when moving from screen to screen

    c) ___ Allowing experienced end users to bypass standard warning messages

    d) ___ Adding hot key functionality

    e) ___ Changing system access to read-only for the accounting department

    f) ___ Moving to a single sign-on process for user authentication

Ranking-order scale questions have a few advantages. They provide comparative data, and they facilitate deeper data-gathering compared with multiple-response items. Data from ranking-order questions indicate what matters most. This type of question also has two disadvantages:

- It practically requires the writer of the question to have perfect knowledge of all possible options, which is not possible.
- False positives may appear in the data. Participants are forced to rank options even if none of the options listed matter to them or reflect their real priorities.

Ranking-order scale questions are useful when:

- It is valuable to have participants compare options.
- Trying to understand a participant's preference for one option compared with options in another question.
- Determining the importance of a particular option compared with options in another question. One survey could ask questions about the importance of certain options, and based on the results of that survey, another survey, in which participants prioritize the options deemed most important, could be developed.
- Determining the usefulness of one option compared with options in another question.
- Determining how urgent it is to implement one option compared with options in another question.
- You would like to know what priority participants would assign each option.

When constructing ranking-order scales, here are some important rules to follow:

- List responses in logical order.
- Include all possible responses.
- Offer at least four or five response options.

CHAPTER 3 Writing Questions

- Include equal numbers of positive and negative statements.
- Make sure response categories don't overlap.
- Use precise wording when possible (e.g., instead of "Often," write "Twice a month").

Specific	Vague
"Less than one time a year"	"Seldom"
"One to 20 times a year"	"Often"
"More than 20 times a year"	"Frequently"

Rating Scales

Rating-scale questions require the participant to assign a value to something, but unlike ranking-order scales, the participant is not required to compare an option with other options in another question.

A *Likert scale item* is a specific type of rating-scale closed-ended question used for assessing attitudes and opinions. Like the ones immediately below, they often offers five response options, such as 1=strongly disagree, 2=disagree, 3=neither agree nor disagree, 4=agree, and 5=strongly agree.

I find the online help useful.	1	2	3	4	5
The user interface flows with my work process.	1	2	3	4	5
I use the hot key functionality.	1	2	3	4	5

Here are additional examples of rating-scale questions:

- What is your level of expertise in each of the following components, where 1=excellent, 2=good, 3=average, 4=fair, and 5=poor?

Product knowledge	1	2	3	4	5
System knowledge	1	2	3	4	5
Technical capabilities	1	2	3	4	5
Organizational understanding	1	2	3	4	5
Industry knowledge	1	2	3	4	5

- Please rate how strongly you agree or disagree with the following statements by circling the appropriate answer, where 1=strongly disagree, 2=disagree, 3=neither agree nor disagree, 4=agree, and 5=strongly agree.

It was easy to learn to use the new system.	1	2	3	4	5
I am better able to complete my work since the new system was implemented.	1	2	3	4	5
The training provided helped me feel confident about using the new system.	1	2	3	4	5
I can find the information I need in the online help.	1	2	3	4	5
It is faster to complete a screen flow in the new system than in the old.	1	2	3	4	5
The new system is easy to use.	1	2	3	4	5

- Please rate how important each of the following is, where 1=very important, 2=important, 3=average importance, 4=slightly important, and 5=not important.

Adhering to privacy regulations	1	2	3	4	5
Complying with Sarbanes-Oxley legislation	1	2	3	4	5
Meeting Americans with Disabilities Act requirements	1	2	3	4	5
Ensuring corporate branding standards are met	1	2	3	4	5
Following corporate security policy	1	2	3	4	5

- Please rate the probability that you will use the following features, where 1=extremely likely, 2=likely, 3=not sure, 4=unlikely, and 5=extremely unlikely.

Online screen-level help	1	2	3	4	5
Online field-level help	1	2	3	4	5
Field-level warning messages	1	2	3	4	5
Field-level error messages	1	2	3	4	5
Hot keys	1	2	3	4	5

CHAPTER 3 Writing Questions

Rating-scale questions take up less room on the page than do most other types of closed-ended questions, and the results can be quickly summarized. They can, however, confuse participants if you change the number of response options from five to eight, or if you change the direction of the scale in a section. Instead, keep the direction of the scale consistent throughout the entire survey.

Rating-scale questions are useful when:

- Determining user satisfaction (e.g., "How easy is the system to use?" Response options would range from "very easy" to "not at all easy.").

- Determining the frequency of an event (e.g., "How often do you use help files?" Options would range from "never" to "every day.").

- Asking participants to self-assess their level of skill or knowledge (e.g., "What do you think your skill level in _____ is? Options could include "incompetent," "competent," and "leading edge." Another question might be "How well-informed do you think you are about health and safety?" Options might include "uninformed," "somewhat informed," and "expert.").

When using rating-scale questions, remember that when there are an uneven number of response options, there will be a natural midpoint—the neutral response. To force participants to express an opinion, offer an even number of answer options.

Some common options for scales are:

- 1=excellent, 2=good, 3=average, 4=fair, and 5=poor
- 1=frequently, 2=often, 3=sometimes, 4=seldom, 5=never
- 1=strongly disagree, 2=disagree, 3=neither agree nor disagree, 4=agree, and 5=strongly agree
- 1=extremely likely, 2=likely, 3=not sure, 4=unlikely, and 5=extremely unlikely
- 1=very important, 2=important, 3=average importance, 4=slightly important, and 5=not important.

When formatting scales, if sufficient space is available, consider writing out each response option in words next to each question. Participants can then circle or check the words rather than the numbers.

Checklist for Writing Good Questions

- Is the question appropriate?
    - Can the purpose of the question be traced back to your objectives?
    - Do you know how the responses will be used?
- Can the question be shortened without losing the meaning?
- Is the wording simple and appropriate for the audience?
- If time is referenced in the question, is the wording clear? For example, a poor question for a survey administered in February would use the phrase "this year." A better question would use the wording "in the past 12 months."
- Is the question too precise, requiring participants to remember specific details from the past?
    - "How many times did you use the online help function in 2006?" is a poor question. An interval closed-ended question would work much better.
    - "What percentage of time did you spend attending training in 2007?" is a poor question. A more effective question is "How many hours did you spend attending training in 2007?"
- Does the question address only one issue, or is it a double-barreled question?
    - "Do you find the salespeople friendly and helpful?" is a poor question. It should be rewritten as two questions:
        - Do you find the salespeople friendly?
        - Do you find the salespeople helpful?

- Does the question use acronyms? Acronyms should be avoided unless all participants will know exactly what they mean.
    - If you use an acronym, define it as part of the question.
- Does the question use jargon? Jargon may not be understood by all participants.
    - "Completely risk-adverse" is poor wording. Better wording is "will not take risks."
    - "Takes calculated risks" is poor wording. "Weighs risks before proceeding" is a possible rewrite.
- Is the question complex or time-consuming? If so, the participant may not take the time to respond or may be put off the entire survey.
- Is the question difficult or mentally taxing? A demanding question would, for example, ask participants to rank 25 options.
    - Difficult questions can tire out even motivated participants; they may not respond or might respond "don't know."
    - When participants don't understand questions, they may answer them incorrectly.
- Is the question too vague? For example, "Have you seen the dentist recently?" is a poor question. What does "recently" mean? A better question is "Have you seen the dentist in the past nine months?"
    - "July and August" is better than "summer"; "2008" is better than "last year"; and "6:00 p.m." is better than "evening."
    - The words "never," "sometimes," "often," and "always" are not specific enough. Rather, define what those responses would mean specifically; this will usually ensure better—more specific—results. For example, they should be defined—e.g., "less than 10 times," "11 to 20 times," and "more than 21 times."
- Does the question use the word "you"? "You" is too vague; it could mean "you and your team" or just "you." Using "you personally" will clarify your meaning.

- Is the question personal? Such questions may seem threatening or offensive.
  - "What is your income?" is one example. It is better to provide a range of response options than to ask this as an open-ended question.
- Does the question suggest a response?
  - "How should professors provide opportunities to students to make up tests they missed due to extended family vacations?" is a poor question. It can be rewritten "What provisions, if any, should professors...."
  - Alternatively, you can use two questions. For example:
    - Should professors provide opportunities to students to make up tests they missed due to extended family vacations? Yes ___ No ___ If yes, please explain.
- Is the wording of the question neutral, to avoid biasing the respondent?
  - For example, a poor question might use adjectives that describe the survey writer's feelings: "hardworking salespeople," "dangerous work environment," or "disgusting advertisement."
- Could the wording of the question lead to prestige bias? *Prestige bias* occurs because participants want to answer in a socially acceptable way.
  - "How much time did you spend helping your children do homework?" could lead to prestige bias. If the participant says "none," does he or she appear to be a good parent? To ask this question, you could use a skip pattern: the first question would be, "Do you help your children do homework? Yes or No?" If the participant answers Yes, ask how much time. You could also offer an open-ended question to provide the participant the opportunity to explain why or why not (e.g., my spouse helps the kids). You could use a question later in the survey to cross-check the response; for example, "What do you do weekdays between 6 and 9 pm?"

CHAPTER 3 Writing Questions

- Does the question contain any *behavioral expectation bias*, meaning that the question leads the participant with an expected response?
  - A poor question would ask, "Most users have used the help file in the past three months. Have you?" This could be rewritten "Have you used the help file in the past three months?"
- Does the question contain loaded words or phrases? *Loaded words* can cause the participant to have immediate positive or negative feelings. Participants may react more to the wording than to the question.
  - For example, "boss" might be a loaded word. A better word might be "leader."
  - If you begin a question with "The business sponsor says...," participants may immediately agree because they trust what the sponsor says, or disagree primarily because they are skeptical about the sponsor.
  - Don't use loaded words or phrases that suggest approval or disapproval.
    - For example, "Many business analysts feel their workload has been unfairly increased. What additional assignments have you been given this year?" is a poor question. A better question is "What responsibilities do you have in addition to business analysis?"
- Does the question contain double negatives? These are confusing to the reader and may affect the quality of the data collected from the question.
  - "I work hard to avoid not meeting my deadlines" is a poorly written item. "I work hard to meet my deadlines" is a good rewrite.
- Is the question ambiguous? Could a word in the question mean different things to different people?
  - For example, "drug use" could mean use of "illegal drugs," "prescription drugs," or "over-the-counter drugs."

- Have terms or concepts been left open for interpretation?
    - For example, "The project office provides the necessary resources to…" is too vague. Better wording is "The project office provides the necessary resources (staff and equipment) to.…"
- Can the question be answered even if the participant has no knowledge of the topic? Such questions can lead to *meaningless responses*.
    - For example, "Do you agree with the organization's policy?" is a poor question. "What is your opinion of X policy?" is better.
- Does the question have the same number of positive and negative options? If not, it has *loaded response categories*.

Good Habits for Writing Questions

- When writing survey questions, remember these tips:
- Use simple words.
- Ensure the wording is appropriate for the audience.
    - Will the group understand the language used?
    - Keep the age and education level of the participants in mind, but do not talk down to participants too much or they may be turned off.
    - Select words participants would use in everyday conversation.
    - Consider asking the pilot group to verify the wording used (see Chapter 5 for more on pilot groups).
- Some participants may exhibit a bias (for example, always agreeing). Word questions so participants must think about the answers. Participants who tend to always agree should have to select "disagree" for some questions in order to consistently endorse a point of view.

- If exploring two sides of an issue, include open-ended questions for each side of the issue. For example:
  - What are the strengths of the system?
  - What are the weaknesses of the system?
- If the results of the survey will be compared with data from another survey, review the wording of questions in the other survey and use the same or similar wording.
- If the survey will be administered more than once, use the exact same wording in both surveys to ensure reliable results. This is especially important if comparing the results of the two surveys.
- If the survey contains questions that direct the participant to do one of two things depending on his or her response, provide clear instruction about what to do next. Questions like these create a *skip pattern*. The use of skip patterns in a survey should be kept to a minimum unless the survey is being administered electronically.[3] Here is an example of a simple skip pattern:

  20. Are you aware of the corporate privacy policy?
      No _____ → Please go to question 32 on the next page.
      Yes _____ → Please continue to question 21.
  21. Have you ever attended ...

Notes

1. If only two response choices are necessary, as long as the question is clear, the data will likely be accurate. But if later it is decided that the responses must be broken down, the business analyst will not be able to do so. The error in that case would be that the survey included an item that didn't yield the necessary data, not that the item yielded erroneous data.
2. Note that these response options do not reflect equal intervals of time. This is not incorrect because the intervals make sense in context and are relevant to the question.
3. Skip patterns are easily handled by today's survey software. When completing surveys electronically, participants will not be aware that they are answering different questions than other participants, and they won't mistakenly follow the wrong pattern.

CHAPTER 4
Ordering and Laying Out the Survey

Once you have finished writing the questions, you must think about the design of the survey. Design elements to consider are:

- Appearance
- The length of the survey
- The order of the questions
- The combination of questions.

Appearance

When a participant first starts the survey, motivate him or her by "creating interest and confidence that they can answer all the questions" (Abbey-Livingston 1982, 44). Questions at the beginning of the survey should be:

- Related directly to the objectives stated in the cover letter
- Relatively easy to answer
- Neutral; don't start with questions that ask for the participant's opinion.

Consider starting with questions that ask for demographic details, which will allow you to get to know the participant, but avoid education or income questions at this point. Consider qualifying the participant at the start of the survey by using a filtering question. A *filtering question* in a web-based survey is used to determine if the participant is qualified to answer one or more subsequent questions. If the "wrong" answer is selected, the participant receives a message expressing appreciation for his or her interest; at that point, the survey ends.

After you have identified the initial questions, arrange the rest of the questions in a logical order. (The section "The Order of the Questions" later in this chapter provides more details.) At the end of the survey, leave the participant with a positive feeling. Ask the participant if he or she has anything further to say with a question such as "Is there anything else you would care to add that has not been adequately addressed in this survey?" And be sure to thank the participant for taking the survey.

It is important to use transitions effectively throughout the survey. *Transitions* indicate that the survey is changing direction. They are frequently used as a bridge to the first set of questions, between sections, at the start of new pages, or to break up a long series of questions. For a minor change in the type of questioning, a short transition is appropriate; if there is a major change in questioning, a longer transition is suggested. Be sure not to use too many transitions—they might cause the participant to lose interest. Sample transitions you might try include:

- "Now, we will change direction slightly and ask about the…"
- "We would like to get your input about related topics. One topic we do not know enough about is…"
- "There are only a few questions left. We want to ask about…"
- "To help summarize the responses and interpret the results, we would like to learn more about you."

Here you would include demographic questions about the participant's team, years of experience in his or her role, what type of system user he or she is, geographic location, level in the organization, and level of technical knowledge. Here's a sample transition addressing two of these data points: "First, I need to ask a few general questions to determine how many systems you are knowledgeable about and how long you have been on this team."

Depending on how the survey will be administered—by email, on paper, or on the web—consider these format-related pointers:

- Use plenty of white space so the survey does not look crowded.
- Assign a unique identifier to each question and option.
- Do not split questions between pages.
- Create an appealing, easy-to-follow layout.
- Ensure spelling and grammar are correct.
- For open-ended questions, be sure to leave enough space for a reply. If you provide only one line, participants will assume you want a very brief answer.
- If certain questions are to be answered by some participants and not others, give clear instructions.

The Length of the Survey

Time is critical in our busy world. The length of the survey can affect the *response rate*, which is the percentage of participants invited to participate in the survey that actually complete the survey. If the survey is too long, participants may get tired and stop. This is called *abandoning the survey*. If the survey has a lot of open-ended questions, it will take longer to complete. Suggested survey lengths vary. If the survey is too short—say, three questions—participants may wonder whether the survey has a real purpose. That said, a short survey should generally contain less than ten questions and take no more than five to ten minutes to complete. A longer survey should not exceed five pages.

The Order of the Questions

The order of the questions in a survey is important. Here are some things to consider:

- Start with easy questions first.
- Limit the number of questions.
- Try to organize the questions in a way that would mirror a conversation with the participant.
- The unwritten rules of conversation also apply to survey questions. In a conversation, each party gets to know the other before asking personal questions. Personal or sensitive questions, such as those about finances or personal habits or problems, should appear later in the survey.
- Group similar questions or questions about the same topic together. This makes it easier for the participants; they won't have to jump from topic to topic.
- Flow questions in a logical order. Questions may go from general to specific, from easy to difficult to answer, or from most important to least important.
- The questions surrounding a question, especially those immediately preceding it, can affect how that question is answered.

Combining Questions

Survey questions can be effectively paired or combined. Consider the following techniques:

- Use a combination of open-ended and closed-ended questions to identify important issues and compare responses.
    - For example, ask a question like "What issues do you think the organization is facing?" Later, ask "In the following list of issues, which two do you think are the most important in our organization?"

CHAPTER 4 Ordering and Laying Out the Survey

- If this technique is used, separate the two questions with other questions.
- Ask the open-ended question first so that participants are not influenced by the options provided in the closed-ended question.
- Analysis of the data can identify what issues participants talk about when they are not prompted, which are top priorities when they are forced to choose, and which appear in both situations.

- Use a funneling technique in the survey. *Funneling* is beginning a section of the survey with an open-ended question, then moving into closed-ended questions about very specific topics.
  - Several funnels can be used in a single survey.
  - The following series of questions illustrates the funneling technique.
    - "How do you like the new system manual?"
    - "In the past three months, how often have you used this manual to complete your work?"

      a) _____ Less than ten times

      b) _____ 11 to 20 times

      c) _____ 21 to 30 times

      d) _____ More than 31 times.

    - Please respond to the following statements, where 1=strongly disagree, 2=disagree, 3=neither agree nor disagree, 4=agree, and 5=strongly agree.

The format of the manual is easy to use.	1	2	3	4	5
The flow of chapters is logical.	1	2	3	4	5
Explanations provided are clear.	1	2	3	4	5
The examples used relate to my day-to-day work.	1	2	3	4	5

- Now we would like to explore the importance of specific sections of the manual. Please rate the importance of the following sections, where 1=very important, 2=important, 3=average importance, 4=slightly important, and 5=not important.

Product overview	1	2	3	4	5
System overview	1	2	3	4	5
Process flows	1	2	3	4	5
Data dictionary	1	2	3	4	5

When the layout of the survey is complete, look at the order of the questions to ensure that questions flow as intended. The flow of questions can also be verified during the pilot. The pilot process is discussed in the next chapter.

CHAPTER 5

Piloting the Survey

Before sending a survey out to participants, the survey should be tested to ensure the questions will work as intended. The best way to test a survey is by piloting it with a subset of participants. Before the pilot, complete a few pre-pilot steps:

- Read each question out loud to make sure the words flow and clearly communicate the intended message. This is especially important if the questions will be asked in an interview setting.
- Verify that skip-pattern questions will make sense to participants. Will the subsequent question to which the participant is directed be meaningful to someone who answered "No" to the previous question?
- Make sure that each question will yield the type of information required. In other words, can you use the results to analyze the data in the manner you planned?
- Review questions with peers to test for validity and understandability.
- Make sure the survey does not have any spelling mistakes or grammatical errors.

Once you have completed these steps, you can conduct the pilot.

The Pilot

The pilot process is an important step that will help you elicit general impressions of the survey. Running a pilot will also allow you to:

- Verify that the questions will deliver the expected results.
- Gather feedback on the layout of the survey.
- Get feedback on the order of questions.
- Verify how long it really takes to complete the survey.
- Obtain feedback on content and wording.
- Determine whether answers may be influenced by response options. When testing a particular question in a pilot, you might include two forms of the question. In the second form, the options would be reversed or randomized.

The pilot can be conducted using the same method used to administer the actual survey. However, if the survey will conducted by mail, email, or online, it may be beneficial to pilot the survey using focus groups or structured interviews. Focus groups or structured interviews provide more opportunity to test the questions. For instance, a multiple-response closed-ended question could be read to the group and the participants asked to write down possible answer choices. When the participants are done, you would reveal the actual response options and compare them with those identified by the group. The additional choices identified by the group might then be added to the list of response options.

During an in-person pilot session, participants can ask questions. Their questions are valuable feedback. Participants can also explain any assumptions they had to make to answer the questions or why certain questions are confusing.

You should watch for nonverbal feedback, too. Are participants skipping questions or erasing and changing answers? You might find out participants are skipping questions during the session if you watch a small group take the survey. If the pilot is conducted by mail, email, or online, it would, of course, be more difficult to get this type of information.

Based on the feedback you gather in the pilot, you can revise the layout and edit the questions or the cover letter before administering the real survey. If you included extra feedback questions in the pilot survey, be sure to remove them before sending out the actual survey.

Selecting the Pilot Participants

The people who participate in the pilot survey should be a representative sample of the target audience for the survey. The pilot participants will not participate in the actual survey. The size of the pilot group will depend on the size of the actual survey group, but usually 10 to 30 people should be asked to participate in the pilot. When deciding who should participate in the pilot, consider three types of people:

1. **Colleagues.** This group can help you determine how well the survey will meet its goals and objectives.

2. **Potential users of the results of the survey.** This group can assess the survey's accuracy.

3. **A cross section of potential participants.** This group will provide initial survey results.

The Cover Letter for the Pilot

The cover letter for the pilot survey will be very similar to the cover letter for the actual survey, though you should include additional information in the cover letter for the pilot:

- An invitation to be part of the pilot.
- Details about how the pilot will be conducted. If it will be a focus group format, provide an agenda.

If the pilot survey will be completed by mail, email, or online, add feedback questions to the end of the survey, preceded by an appropriate transition. Possible feedback questions include:

- What was your general impression of the survey?
- How long did it take you to complete the survey?
- Did the survey cover letter create a positive impression? Yes _____ No _____
- Did the questionnaire create a positive impression? Yes _____ No _____
- Did the cover letter motivate you to reply? Yes _____ No _____
- Was each question clear and easy to understand?
- Were there any questions you did not understand the reason for asking?
- Were there any questions you expected to be asked and were not?
- Does each question measure what it is intended to measure? (This question would work only if your pilot group is composed of colleagues or those who will use the survey results; other potential participants would not know how to answer it.)
- Did you understand all the words in the questions?
- Were any questions confusing? Which ones?
- Did questions seem to repeat themselves? Where?
- Did the questions seem relevant to the problem or issue stated in the introduction?
- What other questions should be asked?
- Was the survey easy to follow?
- Were the instructions easy to understand?

Analyzing the Pilot Results

When analyzing the results, consider the following questions:

- Were the questions interpreted similarly by all participants?
- Were the questions answered correctly?
- Were any questions skipped?
- Are you able to interpret all the answers?
- Does each closed-ended question have an answer option that is appropriate for each participant? If most participants chose "other," the answer options might not be entirely appropriate.

CHAPTER 6

Sending Out the Survey and Following Up with Participants

When the pilot is complete and the final adjustments have been made to your survey, it is time to send it to your list of potential participants. This chapter will discuss the importance of a good cover letter, things to consider when sending out the survey, following up with participants, and finally, survey response rates.

The Importance of the Cover Letter

Every survey should be accompanied by a cover letter. The cover letter should not exceed one page and should precede the questions in the survey. Include a draft version of the cover letter in the pilot survey and gather feedback on it, then edit it as necessary. It's important that the cover letter create a positive impression.

The cover letter should answer the following questions:

- Who is conducting the survey?
- Why is the survey being done?
- What information is being sought?
- How have participants been selected?
- What will be done with the results?
- Are the answers confidential?[1]

- Are the responses anonymous?[2]
- By when must the survey be completed?
- Will participants get information on the survey results?

You may also want to include:

- The name of the group sponsoring the survey
- Contact information so that participants can ask questions
- A statement that makes participants feel as if their participation is important to the success of the survey
- Information on how confidentiality will be preserved if participants provide their names
- A note about any incentives for completing the survey
- Any special instructions for completing the survey.

Participants decide whether to complete a survey based on the value of the survey, the time it will take to complete, and their ability to answer the questions. Make sure all of these points are addressed in the cover letter. (The cover letter can address participants' ability to answer the questions by explaining how and why the participants were selected.)

Here are some tips for writing the cover letter:

- Avoid using phrases such as "Your help is needed" or "Enclosed is a questionnaire." This wording turns people off.
- Focus the cover letter on the participant. Never start the cover letter with "I."
- Don't use "hope" or "hopeful"; use stronger words to encourage recipients to respond.
- Proofread very carefully. Errors look sloppy.

In *Enjoying Research? A "How-To" Manual on Needs Assessment*, Diane Abbey-Livingston and David S. Abbey (146) suggest a useful, simple cover letter format:

CHAPTER 6 Sending Out the Survey and Following Up with Participants

Dear (name):

First paragraph: Define what the survey is about and explain why it is important.

Second paragraph: Explain who the participants are (the types of participants, not their names) and how participants were chosen (for example, by the executive sponsor).

Third paragraph: State whether responses are confidential or anonymous.

Fourth paragraph: Explain how the results will be used.

Last paragraph: Tell participants whether they will get a reward for responding and whether the survey results will be shared with participants, and provide contact information so that participants can ask questions.

Here's a sample cover letter based on this model:

Dear (participant's name):

A survey is being conducted to gather important information from actual users about the organization's workflow tool. You have been selected to participate in the survey. This survey will ask you to evaluate your satisfaction with the current workflow tool and gives you an opportunity to provide feedback about the changes for the next release.

The survey is being sent to a randomly selected group of team leads, tier-one customer service representatives, and tier-two customer service representatives from all departments that use the workflow tool.

Your input is confidential. No personal information will be obtained or recorded.

The information gathered through this survey will be used by senior management as input to finalize the scope of the next release.

You can access the survey through this link: <survey link>. It should take no more than ten minutes to complete. All responses must be received by no later than Monday, April 30.

If you choose to complete the survey, you can be entered into a drawing for a prize. To enter the drawing, please email your name to survey@organizationname.com once you have completed the survey. If you have any questions about the survey, please email survey@organizationname.com.

Thank you for taking part in this survey.

Sending Out the Survey

When the survey is ready to be sent:

- Make sure it is an appropriate time to do a survey. For example, don't send the finance department a survey during year-end.
- Notify participants that they will be asked in the next week to complete a survey, and explain why it is important to participate.
- Send the survey, or an invitation to complete it, early in the week, on Monday or Tuesday.
- Make clear how long the survey will be available. Deadlines may influence the speed of responses but will not influence the response rate.
- If responses are confidential, be sure to store them in a secure location no one but the project team can access.

Following Up with Participants

Following up with participants is an optional step in the survey process. Depending on how the survey is administered, you may not know who the actual participants are. For example, if the survey is online and is accessed through a link on a website, or if the initial group of participants

CHAPTER 6 Sending Out the Survey and Following Up with Participants **67**

is asked to pass the survey on to other people, following up with participants is not feasible.

If the participants are known, you may send a reminder to complete the survey halfway through the time period allowed for completion. Individuals who do not respond after the second reminder are not likely to participate in the survey.

Response Rates

Expect to obtain a response rate somewhere between 10 percent and 40 percent. The response rate may be higher if the survey is conducted within the organization. Participants internal to the organization will have some stake in the results of the project, which may increase the response rate. Management endorsement of the survey may also improve response rates, but be careful: If participants feel pressured to participate, they may not take the survey seriously or think carefully about the answers.

Telephone and one-on-one surveys will have higher response rates than mail-out surveys. One-on-one surveys can yield a response rate of 80 to 90 percent, whereas a mail-out survey may garner a response rate below 50 percent (Palys 1997, 146). Before deciding to conduct a survey, consider the expected response rate and determine if the survey is worthwhile.

Response rates may increase if an incentive is offered to participate. Make sure the cover letter mentions any incentives. If responses are confidential, there must be a method that will allow participants to receive the incentive without compromising their privacy.

Notes

1. *Confidential* means that survey responses will not be linked to identifying information (such as participants' names or other information that would enable the user of the results to figure out who provided the data). The business analyst must make sure results are not broken down in a way that identifies a person's responses (for

example, if there are three men and one woman in Department A, results for that department should not be reported by gender because it would be obvious who the female respondent was and what her answers were).
2. With *anonymous* responses, the business analyst has no way of linking the responses to particular participants. Anonymity is difficult, if not impossible, to guarantee for Internet or email surveys because the IP address the survey response came from can be tracked.

CHAPTER 7

Analyzing and Interpreting the Results

When the survey is closed, the data must be analyzed. This chapter looks at analyzing data from open-ended and closed-ended questions and explains how to use simple statistics.

When planning a survey, make sure you allow enough time to complete analysis. How long analysis will take depends on:

- The total number of survey questions
- The format of the questions; open-ended questions typically take longer to analyze
- The number of participants
- How much experience you have in analyzing and interpreting survey data
- Whether information from the initial analysis prompts further analysis.

As you gain more experience in surveying and analysis, it will be easier to estimate the amount of time needed for analysis and interpretation of the results.

Before starting analysis, review all the data and determine whether you have outlying data, incorrect values, or missing data. *Outlying data* are responses that are not consistent with the rest of the data—for example, if just one of 20 teams surveyed was dissatisfied with the new employee portal. These data should not be excluded from the analysis. They should be analyzed twice: once using all the data from the question, and a second time excluding the outlying data. This will allow you to determine how the outlying data is affecting the results and how to use the results.

Incorrect data are data that do not make sense based on the question asked. Let's say that a survey's target audience is senior citizens, and participants are asked to give their ages. If one participant said that he is 15 years old, that response should be excluded from the analysis because it appears to be incorrect.

When not all participants answer a question, you have *missing data*. If a significant number of participants—say, nine out of ten—answered the question, include the data in the analysis. If a complete set of answers is required for the analysis, the calculations should be done using a sample size of nine instead of ten. If most participants did not answer the question, consider excluding that question from the analysis.

Analyzing Data from Open-Ended Questions

For each open-ended question, look at all the responses and try to identify common types of responses. Group those responses together. Give each group a name and a description, and attach the responses to the group.

The results may contain one-off responses that do not fit into any group. If you believe these responses are important, assign each one its own group. If a response is not important, discard it.

Analyzing Data from Closed-Ended Questions

You can use several different descriptive statistics when analyzing and interpreting closed-ended questions. Regardless of which statistical method you use, be sure to have someone check the results for errors. Let's look at five types of descriptive statistics and when each should be used.

- Frequency distribution
- Mean
- Median
- Mode
- Range.

Frequency Distribution

Frequency distribution identifies the number of times each response appears in the overall data from a question. Let's say we're looking at the results from the question "What was the purpose of your survey?" The responses "Understanding user satisfaction with an existing solution" and "Identifying changes users would like to make to an existing system" were both identified seven times.

What was the purpose of your survey? (Please select all that apply.)

	Number of times response was chosen
Prioritizing requirements	5
Identifying the strengths of an existing solution	2
Identifying the weaknesses of an existing solution	4
Understanding user satisfaction with an existing solution	7
Gathering input for other requirements elicitation activities	4
Identifying potential scope items	6
Identifying changes users would like to make to an existing system	7
Other; please specify	1

The responses obtained from the "Other; please specify" option would first be analyzed like responses to an open-ended question, then would be included in the frequency distribution analysis.

The frequency distribution method is used:

- To identify the most popular responses to a question
- To determine how often each option was selected compared with other options
- To analyze results for dichotomous items, where only two options exist.

Frequency distribution may be used along with another statistic, such as the mean. Combining these two statistics will show the option most often selected and what proportion or percentage of the time it was selected.

Mean

The *mean* is the average of a set of scores. Proportions and percentages are the mean-based values most commonly used in a business environment. A *proportion* is a part of the data divided by the whole. *Percentage* is a proportion multiplied by 100. For the purpose of analyzing survey results, the mean shows the proportion or percentage of time a response option was chosen. The formula for calculating the mean is:

$$\frac{\text{(number of times the option was chosen)}}{\text{(total number of times all options were chosen)}}$$

The results from the question "What was the purpose of your survey?" would look like this:

What was the purpose of your survey? (Please select all that apply.)

	Number of times response was chosen	Percentage of time response was chosen
Prioritizing requirements	5	13.8 percent
Identifying the strengths of an existing solution	2	5.5 percent

Identifying the weaknesses of an existing solution	4	11.1 percent
Understanding user satisfaction with an existing solution	7	19.4 percent
Gathering input for other requirements elicitation activities	4	11.1 percent
Identifying potential scope items	6	16.6 percent
Identifying changes users would like to make to an existing system	7	19.4 percent
Other; please specify	1	3.1 percent
Total	36	

The options selected by a greater percentage of participants may seem to be more important or urgent priorities than those selected less often, but this is not always the case. These results should be combined with the results from a ranking-order question on the same topic to confirm the most important priorities.

Look at other factors before determining the significance of the results. A result may be significant if participants from the same demographic consistently answer a certain question the same way, even if those participants are not a majority. For instance, if all end users of a system answered a question about usability differently than the leadership team, senior management, or supervisors, that finding is important.

The mean should be used:

- When the results are numbers and can be added
- When attributes can be measured using a numerical scale, such as scores from a test
- For dichotomous questions, where users of the results would expect to see results expressed as means
- To summarize results from a closed-ended question
- To summarize the participants' demographics.

Mean is best used when the distribution of data is *symmetric*, meaning that the distribution of responses has the same shape on both sides of the mean. This demonstrates that the mean truly does represent the average response.

Median

The *median* is the point that cuts the distribution of responses in half. Median is sometimes considered the typical response.

When determining the median, if there are an odd number of scores, use the middle point. If there is an even number of scores, take the two middle scores, add them together, and then divide the sum by two to determine the median.

Median may be used in the following situations:

- To identify the typical result or score
- To analyze ordinal data from an interval scale question or a rating-scale question
- If there are a few outlying responses for a question.

Mode

The *mode* is the most frequently occurring score. To determine mode, arrange all scores in order and identify which option occurs most often. Frequency distribution looks at how often each option was selected. The mode identifies which of those was selected the most.

For the question "Learning about which of the following would help improve your use of surveying?", we see that "surveying tools" was selected most often.

Learning about which of the following would help improve your use of surveying? (Please select all that apply.)

	Number of times response was chosen
Surveying tools	8
How to write effective survey questions	7
Types of questions to avoid	6
Types of questions to use	5
How to interpret survey results	4
How to analyze data	4
How to lay out or design a survey	4
Sample questions	1
How to apply survey results	1
Other; please specify	0
The overall survey process	0

Mode may be used in the following situations:

- To show the most popular response.

- For dichotomous items, where only two response options exist.

- When presenting data in a graphic form. This will show the most frequently selected option, compared with the midpoint (median) or the overall average (mean).

The option "other" should rarely be the most frequently selected item. If it is, this indicates that the question lacked appropriate options. Summarize this finding by stating the number of times "other" was selected, and detail the responses participants wrote in. Let's say 200 of 300 participants selected "other" for the question above. Of those 200 participants, 56 specified that they use surveys to determine usability requirements.

Range

The *range* is the distance between the highest and lowest scores in a distribution. This information may be important to understand when presenting data that show the scope of possible results. It also provides a context for a particular numerical response.

Ranges can be used to:

- Show that all participants selected only some of the responses in a wide range.
- Pinpoint the most and least frequently selected options.
- Place a particular result in the context of the full range of possible results. This is particularly useful when presenting data as averages. For example, an average of 2.5 in a range of possible responses from 1 to 5 would be interpreted much differently than an average of 2.5 in a range of 1 to 100.

CHAPTER 8

Reporting on the Results

When the results have been analyzed, it is time to present them to the stakeholders.[1] This chapter explains how to focus the content of your report on the right audience and how to present results in written and presentation format.

Possible Audiences for Survey Results

It is important to determine with whom you will share the survey results. Each group of stakeholders may want different information and a different level of detail. Who might receive a report, and what are they looking for?

Stakeholder category	Information wanted
Decision makers	■ The bottom line
	■ The details that support the results or recommendation
Other executives	■ High-level results or recommendations without the detail
People who will use the results in their work	■ Details and the results or recommendations
People affected by any decisions made using the data	■ The results and the reasons behind the results or recommendations
Participants	■ An overview of high-level results and how the information will be used
	■ Possibly the response rate.

You may also characterize stakeholders by their level of technical interest in the survey:[2]

Audience	Information wanted
Nontechnical	▪ The results, important findings, and how to use those findings ▪ Not interested in data collection methods or statistics and tables
Technical	▪ Details on survey methods, the response rate, and how the sample was chosen ▪ Details of findings; for example, demographic differences found between participants and nonparticipants
Mixed	▪ A balance between technical and nontechnical information.

When you present the findings, you may encounter obstacles that prevent the results from being used. These might include:

Challenge	Underlying cause
Stakeholders do not want to use the results	▪ No ownership of results ▪ Findings conflict with current processes, policies, environment, etc. ▪ No incentive to act on the data ▪ Results are perceived to be inaccurate
Stakeholders don't know how to use the results	▪ Information is at too high a level to be meaningful or useful ▪ Information is too complex
Stakeholders don't know what is expected of them	▪ Results or findings are not linked to a strategic or operational plan ▪ Results are not traced back to the objectives of the survey
Internal barriers	▪ Conflicting priorities ▪ Internal politics.

CHAPTER 8 Reporting on the Results

In addition to deciding who will receive the report, you must decide whether you will use a written report or a presentation to communicate the results. Let's take a look at each format.

The Written Report

Here is a basic outline for a written report. You should tailor the contents of your own report and the order in which you present information based on the interests of the stakeholders who will see it.

1. Title page
   - Title
     - Should be brief and clear
     - Avoid wording like "a report on," "an analysis of," or "the use of"; these terms are dry and overused, and they state the obvious.
   - Authors
   - Sponsors
   - Contributors (anyone who significantly contributed to the purpose, method, or analysis of the survey and who could speak about the survey if asked)
   - The name of the organization
   - Where the survey took place
2. Introduction
   - Why the survey was needed; the problem the survey addressed
   - The objectives of the survey
   - How the survey results will be used
3. Survey characteristics
   - Type of survey (e.g., mail or phone)
   - The contents of the survey
     - Number of questions
     - Description of the content of the questions

- Descriptions of question types (e.g., open-ended, ranking, rating)
- Sample questions
4. Survey methods
    - The design of the survey
    - The sample
        - The number of people invited to participate in the survey
        - The response rate
        - How participants were selected and why this was the best way to select them
        - Potential biases
    - Analysis of data
5. The results
    - A report of data collected in the survey
    - Should be connected to the objective of the survey
6. Conclusions (the interpretation of the data)
    - A summary of important points
    - Comparison of the findings with those gathered in other surveys
7. The meaning of the results and recommendations or next steps
    - Make recommendations only if appropriate; sometimes the results are just data for decision makers to use
8. Appendix
    - The entire contents of the survey, including all questions, or a reference listing for the complete survey.

The Presentation

When presenting your findings to a group, provide the same information as you would in a written report, but at a level of detail appropriate for a presentation. Generally, people can process more information when reading than they can when listening.

Here is a basic outline for a presentation. It can be customized depending on your audience.

1. Introduction
    a. Title
    b. Contributor(s)
    c. Sponsor(s)
    d. Agenda of the presentation
        - Objective of the presentation
        - Questions that will be answered in the presentation
        - An outline of what the audience can expect from the presentation
2. The survey
    a. Background information about the survey, including:
        - Why the survey was done
        - Unique features of the survey (e.g., if it was the first of its kind in the organization)
    b. An overview of the survey
        - Type of survey (e.g., online, telephone)
        - Number of participants and response rate
            ○ How the participants were selected and the characteristics of the sample
        - How long the survey took to complete and how much time was spent preparing it and analyzing the results
        - General contents
            ○ The number of questions
            ○ Types of questions
            ○ One or two sample questions

c. Results
      - A report of data collected in the survey
      - Should be connected to the objective of the survey
   d. Significance of the results; recommendations or next steps
      - Make recommendations only if appropriate; sometimes the results are just data for decision makers to use.

If you are creating a slide show for your presentation, consider these tips:

- Use one slide for each main concept in the presentation.
- Allow one or two minutes to explain each slide.
- Keep the information you share simple. Do not put all the details in the presentation; if necessary, make handouts with more information.
    - Unless you will refer to the handout during the presentation, wait until the end of the presentation to distribute the handout.
    - Include contact information in the handout.
- Keep slides brief. The audience will be listening to you and should not have to spend time reading slides. Slides should contain:
    - No more than eight lines of text
    - No more than six or seven words per line
    - A maximum of ten words per idea.
- Discuss every point on every slide.
- To emphasize points, use numbers, bullets, underscoring, or a contrasting color.
- Do not use more than four colors on a single slide.
- Do not mix fonts.
- Carefully reread text to make sure it is grammatically consistent.
- Use complete sentences.

CHAPTER 8 Reporting on the Results

- Round numbers to whole numbers. If you must use decimals, round to the nearest tenth—e.g., 3.2 percent, not 3.21 percent.
- Tables should have no more than five rows and six columns. It is difficult to see the data in tables with more cells.
- Clearly label all charts and graphs.
- Limit the use of graphics, animation, or sound. These can overwhelm the audience.
- Ask a peer to read through the presentation and give feedback.
- Be sure to review and practice the presentation ahead of time.

Formatting the Results

These are the most common ways to present survey findings:

- Lists
- Pie charts
- Bar charts and line charts
- Tables.

It is best to use more than one of these formats in a report.

Lists

Lists are easy for the reader to follow. When writing lists, keep the following suggestions in mind:

- Use short phrases or sentences to communicate each idea.
  - Be consistent; use all short phrases or all short sentences.
- Start with the same part of speech for all similar items.
- Use consistent capitalization and punctuation or no punctuation at all.

- Leave spaces between items for easier reading.
- Use bullets to denote list items, and use them consistently for the entire list.
- In a presentation, put no more than four items in a list.
- In a written report, put no more than eight items in a list.

Pie Charts

Pie charts show data as a portion of the whole (Figure 8-1). They are best used to present percentages or proportions. Use a pie chart only if the data total 100 percent.

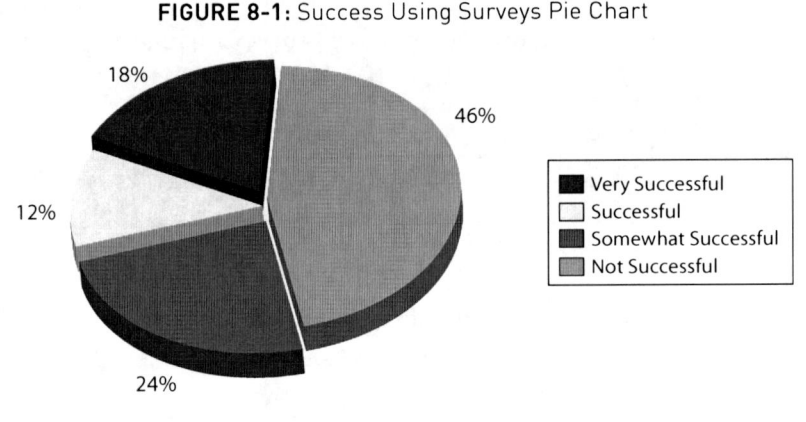

FIGURE 8-1: Success Using Surveys Pie Chart

A pie chart must note the source of the data. If data from another survey are used in the chart, that survey must be cited. If the data are not public, you must secure permission from the author to use the data.

When presenting data in a pie chart, emphasize a specific slice by making it darker or lighter in color than the other slices. If you are comparing data from two surveys, and a particular data element has increased between the two surveys, point out the difference by making one chart larger.

When creating pie charts:

- Use a short title. Use a subtitle if further explanation is needed.
- Do not put more than eight slices in each pie chart. If more than eight slices are needed, group the smallest ones and label them "other."
- When presenting a pie chart, be sure to explain it. Do not assume the audience will understand it.

Bar Charts and Line Charts

Bar charts (Figure 8-2) and line charts (Figure 8-3) work well when you are comparing groups of information or would like to show a change over time. They are easy to read and interpret. All charts should have a title and clearly labeled axes, and the source of the data must be noted.

The y-axis is the vertical axis and shows the dependent variable, such as dollar amount, score, or number of participants. The x-axis is the horizontal axis, and the associated variable can be almost anything, such as names, years, or times of day.

Use bar charts and line charts carefully. Make sure the charts do not suggest that unimportant findings are important. If the difference between findings is not important, note that it is not significant.

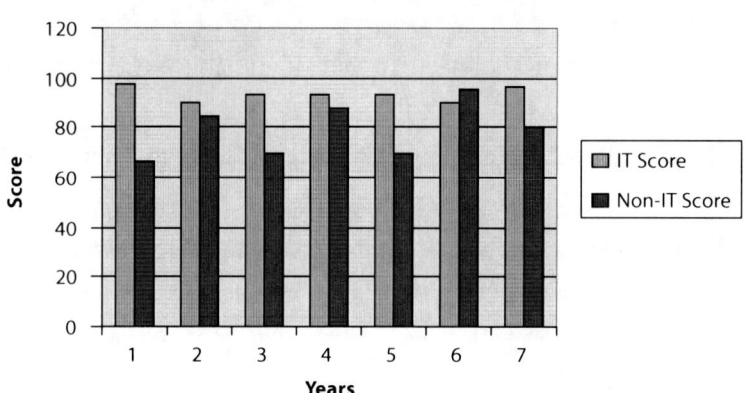

FIGURE 8-2: Job Satisfaction Bar Chart

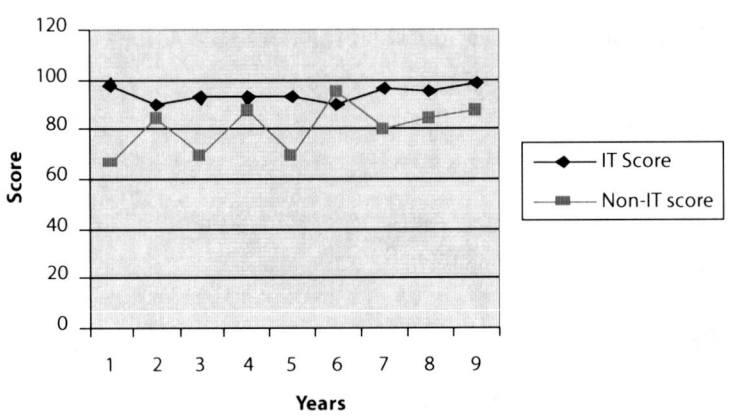

FIGURE 8-3: Job Satisfaction Line Chart

Here are some guidelines for preparing bar charts and line charts:

- If more than six or seven bars are required, use a horizontal chart instead of a vertical chart.
- If showing year-over-year changes, consider showing every other year instead of all years.
- If the value zero is not the starting point, clearly point out the starting value to the reader.
- Note the context of the survey (e.g., at which organization it was conducted).
- Include a legend.
- Use a line chart instead of a bar chart if you are comparing many points in time.
- Use notes to explain whether the differences in data values are significant.
- Explain all bar charts or line charts when presenting them. Do not assume the audience will understand them.

Tables

Tables are more effective in written reports than they are in presentations because they take time to review and absorb. They are useful when summarizing data about participants and their responses.

When creating tables:

- Decide which variables are most important to show or compare, and make them the column headings (e.g., members vs. nonmembers).
- Report values in descending order.

Notes

1. Portions of this chapter were adapted with permission from Arlene Fink, *How to Report on Surveys* (Thousand Oaks, CA: Sage Publications, 2002).
2. Ibid., p. 27.

APPENDIX A

A Checklist for Writing Good Questions

- Is the question appropriate?
- Can the purpose of the question be traced back to your objectives?
- Do you know how the responses will be used?
- Can the question be shortened without losing the meaning?
- Is the wording simple and appropriate for the audience?
- If time is referenced in the question, is the wording clear?
- Is the question too precise, requiring participants to remember specific details from the past?
- Does the question address only one issue, or is it a double-barreled question?
- Does the question use acronyms?
- Does the question use jargon?
- Is the question complex or time-consuming?
- Is the question difficult or mentally taxing?
- Is the question too vague?
- Does the question use the word "you"? Using "you personally" will clarify your meaning.
- Is the question personal?
- Does the question suggest a response?

- Is the wording of the question neutral, to avoid biasing the respondent?
- Could the wording of the question lead to prestige bias?
- Does the question contain any behavioral expectation bias, meaning that the question leads the participant with an expected response?
- Does the question contain loaded words or phrases?
- Does the question contain double negatives?
- Is the question ambiguous?
- Have terms or concepts been left open for interpretation?
- Can the question be answered even if the participant has no knowledge of the topic?
- Does the question have the same number of positive and negative options?

APPENDIX B
Survey Process Template

An overall process template or checklist like the one below could help users keep track of each step of the survey process.

Survey Component	Notes
Choose survey type	Self-administered
	Group-administered
	Mailed
	Telephone
	One-on-one interview
	Focus group
Define objectives	Use a mind mapping tool
Identify stakeholders	Use a stakeholder worksheet
Select participants	Systematic (random) sample
	Convenience sample
	Snowball sample
	Unrestricted sample
	Recruited sample
Define a desired response rate	
Define the number of participants required	
List potential participants	
List pilot participants	

Survey Component	Notes
Check overall layout and appearance	
Create cover letter for pilot	
Identify pilot feedback questions	
Create cover letter	
Determine follow-up method	
Decide whether to offer an incentive to participants	
Analysis	Identify the type of planned analysis, check for outlying data, incorrect values, and missing data. Additional analysis will depend on the actual results.
Report audience	
Determine written report contents	Title page Authors Sponsors Contributors Name of organization Location of survey Introduction Survey characteristics Survey methods (e.g., design of survey, sample, analysis of data) Results Results analysis and conclusions Recommended next steps Appendixes

APPENDIX C
Question-Writing Template

Question Number	
Question Objective	
Question Type	
Question Wording	
Pilot Feedback	
Revised Wording	
Plans for Analysis	

Two example questions follow:

Question Number	1
Question Objective	Demographic
Question Type	Multiple response item
Question Wording	Please indicate your position in the organization: ■ Team lead ■ Tier-one customer service representative ■ Tier-two customer service representative
Pilot Feedback	None
Revised Wording	Not required
Plans for Analysis	Total number respondents by position Mean by position Report using only the mean

Question Number	2
Question Objective	Overall satisfaction or dissatisfaction with workflow tool
Question Type	Rating scale
Question Wording	Please rate how strongly you agree or disagree with the following statements by circling the appropriate box, where: | 1 =	Strongly Agree
2 =	Agree
3 =	Neither Agree or Disagree
4 =	Disagree
5 =	Strongly Disagree | - The workflow tool is easy to use. - The information available to me when completing a work request is acceptable. - The training provided helped me feel confident using the workflow tool. - My ability to complete my work has improved since the workflow tool was implemented.
Pilot Feedback	None
Revised Wording	Not required
Plans for Analysis	Mean based on number of respondents answering disagree and strongly disagree Look at responses by position to determine any trends

APPENDIX D
Case Study

This case study is organized in the same order as the book. It is intended to demonstrate the survey process at work. The case study begins with background information, then covers the eight steps of the survey process.

The company this case study focuses on, XYZ, is in the financial sector and is a large organization with more than 8,000 employees. It operates in North America only. Three years ago, all customer service teams in the organization began using a process workflow tool. Although minor improvements have been made to this tool over the past three years, no significant changes have been implemented.

The organization is now planning a major upgrade to this system and has asked employees for input, which will be used to make decisions about the scope of the upgrade. The company has administered two separate surveys: one for senior management and a second for people who use the workflow tool daily. This case study addresses the second survey.

XYZ has a two-tier customer service structure. Tier-one work requests are simple. They can be completed by one person with comprehensive product knowledge. Tier-two work requests are more complex and require multiple people with product expertise and some decision-making authority to complete the work.

The workflow management tool is a complex system with the following functionality:

- Daily dashboard reporting on:
    - Service-level statistics by product, work role, service tier, and team
    - Backlog of work requests by product, service tier, and team
- Ability to direct work requests through work queues based on date of work request, product, type of request, language of request, and role required to complete the request
- Step-by-step processing for simple work requests, complete with job aids, process information, and supplementary documentation
- Step-by-step processing for complex work requests with process information, but limited job aids and supplementary information
- Ability to move a work request from one role to another role within a process flow based on which role should complete the step
- Ability to assign "follow-up" status to work requests when waiting for additional information
- Ability to show customers the status of work requests via a web interface.

The organization used the eight-step survey process outlined in this book. The user survey was administered online using a Zoomerang purchased package. The purchased package was used instead of the free tool because the survey included skip patterns. This functionality was not available in the free version.

Defining the Objectives

The survey process began with defining the objectives of the survey. XYZ identified two objectives:

APPENDIX D Case Study

- To evaluate the satisfaction of employees who use the workflow tool on a daily basis. These employees include team leaders responsible for meeting service-level standards and customer service representatives who complete the work requests.
- To understand what changes would most benefit employees in the next upgrade of the workflow tool.

Each objective was deconstructed into many variables and variations. Each variable and variation was further analyzed. An assessment was conducted to determine which of these variables and variations should be included in the survey to best achieve its objectives and provide the desired information.

For the first objective, evaluating employee satisfaction with the workflow tool, questions were based on the following variables:

- Satisfaction with specific elements
- Dissatisfaction with specific elements
- Satisfaction with:
  - Usability
  - Content
    - Level of detail in process information
    - Level of detail in job aids
    - Level of detail in supplementary information
    - Ability to find or access content
  - Training
    - Timing of training
    - Level of detail
    - Format

- Amount of training
- Helpfulness with regard to day-to-day tasks
  ○ Job satisfaction with workflow tool
    - Improvement in day-to-day work
    - Increase in professionalism. (e.g., If the users previously operated in a paper-based manual environment (outdated) and now operate in an environment with technology, do they feel more professional?)

For the second objective, identifying improvements that should be considered for the upgrade, questions were based on the following variables:

- New areas of content
- Usability of the existing system
- Customer service representatives' interest in specific new features, such as:
  ○ Calculator tools
  ○ Ability to email customers directly from the tool interface
  ○ Ability to import documents and attach them to a work request
  ○ Ability to combine two work requests into a single work request when appropriate
  ○ Ability to temporarily stop a work request to answer the phone, then begin a different work request.

Team leads were asked the questions above, as well as three questions about their interest in the following possible new features:

- Reporting on the average amount of time to complete each type of work request, by product
- Reporting on the average amount of time to complete each work request, by customer service representative

- Reporting on the range of time to complete each type of work request, by product
- Real-time data on backlogged queues so that resources can be redirected to work on those queues
- Daily statistics on work completed by individual customer service representatives.

Although senior management requested additional questions, the business analyst team was careful to manage scope creep by ensuring that any additional questions traced back to one of the two objectives.

Identifying the Stakeholders

Once the objectives, variables, and variations were understood, the team set about completing analysis on stakeholders and identifying the potential participants. Some preliminary stakeholder analysis had been completed at the start of the requirements effort. After the objectives of the survey were defined, additional analysis identified the following stakeholders:

- **Senior management:** Although this group did not participate in the user survey, it will use the results to determine which enhancements may be made in the next upgrade. Senior management will consider the results of the survey and cost per feature to finalize scope. Senior management paid for the cost of the survey.
- **Training team:** This team plans to use some of the findings to improve its training programs for the workflow tool.
- **Process owners from each department:** This team intends to use the findings to plan future enhancements to content within the workflow tool.
- **Project team:** This team will use the findings from the survey and subsequent decisions to finalize the scope of the next upgrade. Results of the survey will also be used as input for subsequent elicitation activities.

- **Team leads:** The day-to-day work for this group will change based on what is implemented in the next upgrade.
- **Employees using the workflow tool:** The day-to-day work for this group will change based on what is implemented in the next upgrade.

Identifying and Selecting Potential Participants

The stakeholder list was then further categorized to identify potential participant groups. This categorization revealed that the potential participants included team leads, tier-one customer service representatives, and tier-two customer service representatives. The potential participants were segmented into two groups: customer service representatives and team leads. Team leads were asked additional questions in the survey.

Given the size of the organization and the number of employees in customer service representative and team lead roles, a sample of the population participated in the survey. Employees from the following customer service departments were included in the survey on a proportional basis:

- Individual life and health insurance
- Individual savings and retirement
- Group life and health insurance
- Group retirement savings.

Within the customer service departments, employees were further identified and selected, on a proportional basis, based on the following criteria:

- Primary language in which they provide customer service. The languages are English, French, and Spanish.
- Length of time employed in the customer service department.

The survey did not distinguish employees by employment status (permanent full-time, permanent part-time, temporary full-time, or temporary part-time).

The business analysts on the project wanted to receive 100 responses. Because the survey was internal and employees were somewhat motivated to participate, the business analyst team expected a high response rate (close to 40 percent). Senior management emphasized the importance of participation, and a small incentive, gift certificates for a local mall, was offered to participants. To achieve the desired response rate, the business analyst team sent the survey to 330 potential participants. Of the 330 surveys sent out, 200 surveys, or 61 percent, were completed.

Writing the Survey Questions

Once the potential participants were identified and categorized, the business analysts set about writing the survey questions. Because the participants were employees of the organization and had knowledge about the content of the survey, transitions were not used between sections. The team felt that they were not necessary because participants would not be surprised when a new section began. Based on the stated objectives and variables, the following questions were developed for the survey.

Demographic Questions

The survey began with several demographic questions: three multiple-response closed-ended questions and one interval-scale closed-ended question. The demographic information was used to understand differences in responses.

1. What is your position in the organization?

    a) ____ Team lead

    b) ____ Tier-one customer service representative

    c) ____ Tier-two customer service representative

2. In which department do you work?

    a) ____ Individual life and health insurance

    b) ____ Individual savings and retirement

    c) ____ Group life and health insurance

    d) ____ Group retirement savings

3. What is the primary language in which you provide customer service?

    a) ____ English

    b) ____ French

    c) ____ Spanish

4. How long have you have been employed in the customer service department?

    a) ____ Less than one year

    b) ____ One to two years

    c) ____ Three to four years

    d) ____ Five years or more

Questions Related to the First Objective

To evaluate the satisfaction of employees who use the workflow tool on a daily basis, the team asked both closed-ended and open-ended questions. Although the business analysts originally planned to include only closed-ended questions, they decided to add two open-ended questions to determine whether there were other areas of satisfaction or dissatisfaction they were not aware of.

Because this objective dealt with satisfaction, the team wanted to understand participants' opinions. Rating-scale closed-ended questions were perfect for this situation. The rating scale used was 5=strongly disagree, 4=disagree, 3=neutral, 2=agree, 1=strongly agree.

These are the questions related to the first objective of the survey.

1. What do you like most about the workflow tool?

    What do you like least about the workflow tool?

APPENDIX D Case Study

2. Please rate how strongly you agree or disagree with the following statements by circling the appropriate number, where 5=strongly disagree, 4=disagree, 3=neutral, 2=agree, 1=strongly agree.

The workflow tool is easy to use.	1	2	3	4	5
The information available to me when I am completing a work request is acceptable.	1	2	3	4	5
The training provided helped me feel confident about using the workflow tool.	1	2	3	4	5
My ability to complete my work has improved since the workflow tool was implemented.	1	2	3	4	5

3. Please rate how strongly you agree or disagree with the following statements by circling the appropriate number, where 5=strongly disagree, 4=disagree, 3=neutral, 2=agree, 1=strongly agree.

The process flow takes me through each step in a logical order.	1	2	3	4	5
The tool moves from one screen to the next screen quickly.	1	2	3	4	5
Screens are easy to read.	1	2	3	4	5
Screens are laid out logically for the way I complete my work.	1	2	3	4	5
I am taken only to screens I need to use within a work request.	1	2	3	4	5

4. In what ways does the current process documentation meet your needs?

   In what ways does the current process documentation not meet your needs?

5. Please rate how strongly you agree or disagree with the following statements by circling the appropriate number, where 5=strongly disagree, 4=disagree, 3=neutral, 2=agree, 1=strongly agree.

Process information includes all the detail I need to complete a work request.	1	2	3	4	5
Job aids include all the detail I need to complete a work request.	1	2	3	4	5

Supplementary information includes all the detail I need to complete a work request.	1	2	3	4	5
The content I need to complete a work request is easy to find.	1	2	3	4	5

6. Please rate how strongly you agree or disagree with the following statements by circling the appropriate number, where 5=strongly disagree, 4=disagree, 3=neutral, 2=agree, 1=strongly agree.

Training was provided when I needed it.	1	2	3	4	5
The trainer explained concepts I did not understand.	1	2	3	4	5
I received the right amount of information in training to help me do my job.	1	2	3	4	5
The training approach met my needs as an adult learner.	1	2	3	4	5

7. Please rate how strongly you agree or disagree with the following statements by circling the appropriate number, where 5=strongly disagree, 4=disagree, 3=neutral, 2=agree, 1=strongly agree.

The workflow tool has improved my day-to-day work.	1	2	3	4	5
The workflow tool has increased the professionalism of the customer service representative role.	1	2	3	4	5

Questions Related to the Second Objective

To determine which changes would most benefit employees in the next upgrade of the workflow tool, the business analyst team wrote three types of questions about possible scope items.

1. *Multiple-response items* were used to determine features participants wanted to see in the next release.
2. *Rating-scale closed-ended questions* were used to understand how important each possible scope item was to participants. The rating

scale used was 5=not important, 4=slightly important, 3=average importance, 2= important, and 1=very important.

3. ***Ranking-order closed-ended questions*** allowed participants to prioritize three possible scope items.

The following are a sample of the questions related to the second objective of the survey. Participants were asked to select, rate the importance of, and rank proposed content improvements, usability improvements, and new features.

Which of the following content improvements would you like to see in the next release? Please select all that apply.

    a) ___ New types of simple work requests

    b) ___ More supplemental information for simple work requests

    c) ___ Better job aids for simple work requests

    d) ___ Enhanced process information for simple work requests

    e) ___ New types of complex work requests

    f) ___ More supplemental information for complex work requests

    g) ___ Better job aids for complex work requests

    h) ___ Enhanced process information for complex work requests

    i) ___ Other; please specify _____

Please rate the importance of each of the following content improvements, where 5=not important, 4=slightly important, 3=average importance, 2= important, and 1=very important.

New types of simple work requests	1	2	3	4	5
More supplemental information for simple work requests	1	2	3	4	5
Better job aids for simple work requests	1	2	3	4	5
Enhanced process information for simple work requests	1	2	3	4	5
New types of complex work requests	1	2	3	4	5

More supplemental information for complex work requests	1	2	3	4	5
Better job aids for complex work requests	1	2	3	4	5
Enhanced process information for complex work requests	1	2	3	4	5

Please rank your top three priorities for content improvements from 1 to 3, with 1 being your top priority.

    a) _____ New types of simple work requests

    b) _____ More supplemental information for simple work requests

    c) _____ Better job aids for simple work requests

    d) _____ Enhanced process information for simple work requests

    e) _____ New types of complex work requests

    f) _____ More supplemental information for complex work requests

    g) _____ Better job aids for complex work requests

    h) _____ Enhanced process information for complex work requests

If the background of every screen was changed from black to white would you be for _____ or against _____ the change?

Which of the following usability improvements would you like included in the next release? Please select all that apply.

    a) _____ Hot key functionality

    b) _____ Additional warning messages to prevent errors

    c) _____ Streamlined workflow for experienced users

    d) _____ Spell checker for user to user messages

    e) _____ Ability for users to provide on-line feedback during a work request

APPENDIX D Case Study

    f) _____ Ability to change language of work request during the workflow

    g) _____ Other; please specify _____

Please rate how important each of the following usability improvements are where 5 = not important, 4 = slightly important, 3 = average importance, 2 = important, and 1 = very important.

Hot key functionality	1	2	3	4	5
Additional warning messages to prevent errors	1	2	3	4	5
Streamlined workflow for experienced users	1	2	3	4	5
Spell checker for user to user messages	1	2	3	4	5
Ability for users to provide online feedback during a work request	1	2	3	4	5
Ability to change language of work request during the workflow	1	2	3	4	5

Please rank your top three priorities, for usability improvements, from 1 to 3 with 1 being your top priority.

    a) _____ Hot key functionality

    b) _____ Additional warning messages to prevent errors

    c) _____ Streamlined workflow for experienced users

    d) _____ Spell checker for user to user messages

    e) _____ Ability for users to provide on-line feedback during a work request

    f) _____ Ability to change language of work request during the workflow

Which of the following new features would you like to see in the next release? Please select all that apply.

    a) _____ Calculator tools

    b) _____ Ability to email customers directly from the tool

c) _____ Ability to import a document and attach it to a work request

d) _____ Ability to combine two work requests into a single work request when appropriate

e) _____ Ability to temporarily stop a work request to answer the phone, then begin a different work request

f) _____ Other; please specify _____

Please rate how important each of these possible new features is where 5=not important, 4=slightly important, 3=average importance, 2= important, and 1=very important.

Calculator tools	1	2	3	4	5
Ability to email customers directly from the tool	1	2	3	4	5
Ability to import a document and attach it to a work request	1	2	3	4	5
Ability to combine two work requests into a single work request when appropriate	1	2	3	4	5
Ability to temporarily stop a work request to answer the phone, then begin a different work request.	1	2	3	4	5

Please rank your top three priorities for new features from 1 to 3, with 1 being your top priority.

a) _____ Calculator tools

b) _____ Ability to email customers directly from the tool

c) _____ Ability to import a document and attach it to a work request

d) _____ Ability to combine two work requests into a single work request when appropriate

e) _____ Ability to temporarily stop a work request to answer the phone, then begin a different work request.

APPENDIX D Case Study **109**

Which of the following new features would you like included in the next release? Please select all that apply.

    a) _____ Reporting on average amount of time to complete each type of work request by product

    b) _____ Reporting on average amount of time to complete each type of work request by customer service representative

    c) _____ Range of time to complete each type of work request by product

    d) _____ Real time data on which queues are backlogged so resources can be redirect to work on those queues

    e) _____ Daily statistics by customer service representatives on work completed

    f) _____ Other; please specify _____

Please rate how important each of the new features are where 5 = not important, 4 = slightly important, 3 = average importance, 2 = important, and 1 = very important.

Reporting on average amount of time to complete each type of work request by product	1	2	3	4	5
Reporting on average amount of time to complete each type of work request by customer service representative	1	2	3	4	5
Range of time to complete each type of work request by product	1	2	3	4	5
Real time data on which queues are backlogged so resources can be redirect to work on those queues	1	2	3	4	5
Daily statistics by customer service representatives on work completed	1	2	3	4	5

Please rank your top three priorities, for new features, from one to three with one being your top priority.

    a) _____ Reporting on average amount of time to complete each type of work request by customer service representative

    b) _____ Real time data on which queues are backlogged so resources can be redirect to work on those queues

    c) _____ Daily statistics by customer service representatives on work completed

    d) _____ Reporting on average amount of time to complete each type of work request by product

    e) _____ Range of time to complete each type of work request by product

Organizing the Survey

Once the questions were written, the business analyst team began working on the organization and layout of the survey. The survey began with four demographic questions to allow the business analyst team to get to know the participants. Next were the seven questions related to the first objective. The survey ended with 13 questions pertaining to the second objective. Three of the questions for the second objective were answered only by team leads. Based on participants' answers to the first demographic question, which identified their positions in the organization, skip logic was used to ensure that only team leads answered the last three survey questions.

The Pilot

When the questions were written and the layout complete, the business analysts conducted a small pilot with 20 people.

- Five people were the other business analysts on the team.

- Five people were stakeholders who will use the information: the project sponsor, process owners, and the project team.
- Ten people were a representation of the sample of users.

The expected response rate was two to eight responses from the pilot group. In addition to the survey questions, the pilot group was asked the following questions at the end of the survey. These questions were preceded by a transition:

The survey has been completed. Please answer the following five questions to provide feedback on the survey.

The five questions were:

- What was your general impression of the survey?
- How long did it take you to complete the survey?
- Was each question clear and easy to understand?
- Were there any questions you did not understand the reason for asking?
- Were there any questions you expected to be asked and were not?

The cover letter for the pilot was identical to the letter sent with the actual survey but included these additional paragraphs:

> *Conducting a test of a survey with a smaller group is part of the survey process. We would appreciate it if you would participate in this pilot process.*
>
> *In addition to completing the survey, we would like you to provide feedback on both the content of the survey and its presentation. We have included five feedback questions at the end of the survey.*

Ten people responded to the pilot, and only minor adjustments were made to the survey based on the feedback received.

Sending Out the Survey

The departments that would be affected by the upcoming changes to the workflow tool were aware that a survey was going to be conducted; a memo had previously been sent to all employees telling them about the project and requesting their participation if asked.

The cover letter for the survey read as follows:

> A survey is being conducted to gather important information from users about the organization's workflow tool. You have been selected to participate in the survey. This survey will ask you to evaluate your satisfaction with the current workflow tool and will give you an opportunity to provide input about the changes for the next release. The information gathered will be used by senior management as input to finalize the scope of the next release.
>
> The survey has been sent to a randomly selected group of team leads, tier-one customer service representatives, and tier-two customer service representatives from all departments that use the workflow tool. Your input is confidential. No personal information will be collected or recorded.
>
> You can access the survey through <survey link>. It should take no more than ten minutes to complete. All responses must be received no later than Monday, April 30.
>
> If you choose to complete the survey, you can be entered into a drawing for a prize. If you would like to enter the drawing, please email your name to survey@organizationname.com once you have completed the survey.
>
> If you have any questions about the survey, please email survey@organizationname.com.
>
> Thank you for taking part in this survey.

A reminder was sent to participants halfway through the survey period. As mentioned earlier, 61 percent, or 200, of the 330 surveys sent out were completed.

Analysis of the results is below. After the analysis, the intended reporting for the question is shown for most questions. The reporting information appeared in several different formats, including a presentation and two different written reports. The actual reports have not been developed for this case study.

Results: Demographics

1. What is your position in the organization?

Results by position in the organization

Position	Number of participants	Percentage of participants
Team Lead	25	12%
Tier-one CSR	120	60%
Tier-two CSR	55	28%

Reporting

Position	Percentage of participants
Team Lead	12%
Tier-one CSR	60%
Tier-two CSR	28%

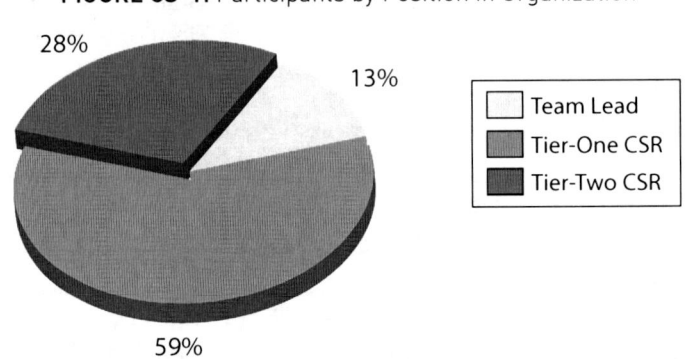

FIGURE CS-1: Participants by Position in Organization

2. In which department do you work?

Results by department

	Team lead	Tier-one CSR	Tier-two CSR
Total number of participants	25	120	55
Individual life and health insurance	5	35	10
Percentage of participants	20.0%	29.2%	18.2%
Individual savings and retirement	3	25	10
Percentage of participants	12.0%	20.8%	18.2%
Group life and health insurance	6	45	5
Percentage of participants	24.0%	37.5%	9.1%
Group retirement savings	11	15	30
Percentage of participants	44.0%	12.5%	54.5%

CSR = Customer service representative

APPENDIX D Case Study

Reporting

The following chart shows departmental representation for the respondents.

	Team lead	Tier-one CSR	Tier-two CSR
Individual life and health insurance	20.0%	29.2%	18.2%
Individual savings and retirement	12.0%	20.8%	18.2%
Group life and health insurance	24.0%	37.5%	9.1%
Group retirement savings	44.0%	12.5%	54.5%

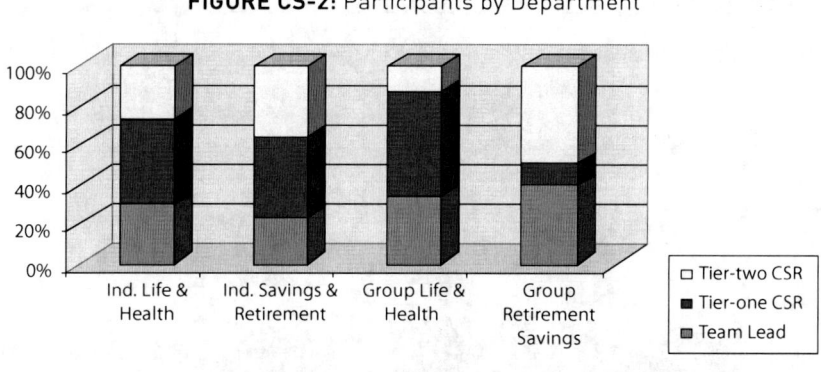

FIGURE CS-2: Participants by Department

3. *What is the primary language in which you provide customer service?*

Results by language

	Team lead	Tier-one CSR	Tier-two CSR
Total number of participants	25	120	55
English	15	85	40
Percentage of participants	60.0%	70.8%	72.7%

	Team lead	Tier-one CSR	Tier-two CSR
French	6	25	10
Percentage of participants	24.0%	20.8%	18.2%
Spanish	4	10	5
Percentage of participants	16.0%	8.4%	9.1%

Reporting

The following chart shows representation by primary language for the respondents.

	Team Lead	Tier-one CSR	Tier-two CSR
English	60.0%	70.8%	72.7%
French	24.0%	20.8%	18.2%
Spanish	16.0%	8.4%	9.1%

The results for question 3 accurately represent the actual population of the customer service centers.

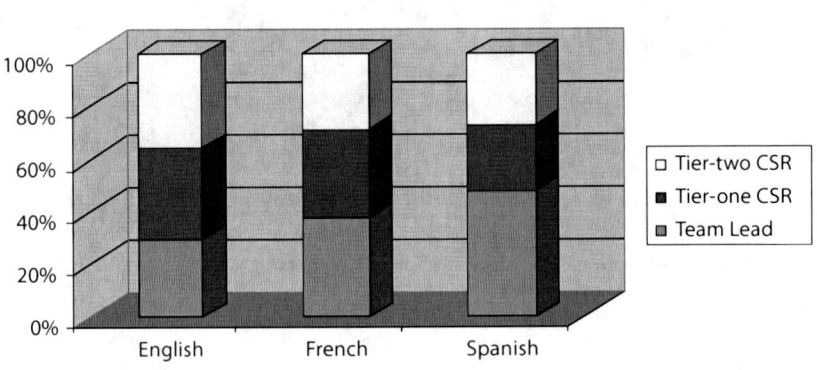

FIGURE CS-3: Participants by Primary Language

APPENDIX D Case Study

4. How long have you been employed in the customer service department?

Results by years of experience

	Team Lead	Tier-one CSR	Tier-two CSR
Number of participants	25	120	55
Less than one year	2	45	3
Percentage of participants	8.0%	37.5%	5.5%
One to two years	0	50	7
Percentage of participants	0.0%	41.7%	12.7%
Three to four years	4	20	15
Percentage of participants	16.0%	16.7%	27.3%
Five years or more	19	5	30
Percentage of participants	76.0%	4.1%	54.5%

Reporting

The following chart shows representation by years of experience in the customer service department for the respondents.

	Team Lead	Tier-one CSR	Tier-two CSR
Less than one year	8.0%	37.5%	5.5%
One to two years	0.0%	41.7%	12.7%
Three to four years	16.0%	16.7%	27.3%
Five years or more	76.0%	4.1%	54.5%

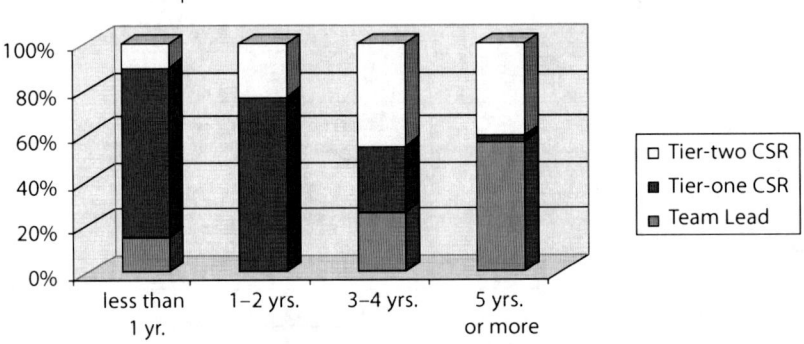

FIGURE CS-4: Participants by Years of Experience in the Customer Service Department

Results: The First Objective

Here are the responses that were reported for the first question related to the first objective, evaluating satisfaction with the workflow tool.

1. *What do you like most about the workflow tool?*

   - The ability to better manage my team's workloads.
   - It makes me feel better able to do a good job.
   - The training is really good, and I started working feeling that I could do the job.
     - Further analysis shows 90 percent of participants with this response are tier-one CSRs with two years or less of experience.

What do you like least about the workflow tool?

   - There is not enough information in job aids to complete the process without a lot of experience.
     - Further analysis shows 82 percent of participants with this response are tier-two CSRs with four years or less of experience.

APPENDIX D Case Study

- Processes for complex work requests do not have enough information.
    - 98 percent of participants who stated this are tier-two CSRs who work on complex work requests. This result was anticipated, because 90 percent of complex tier-two work requests do not have complete process information.
- I have to go outside the tool to email customers with updates.

2. ***Please rate how strongly you agree or disagree with the following statements by circling the appropriate number.*** The rating scale used was 5=strongly disagree, 4=disagree, 3=neutral, 2=agree, 1=strongly agree.

	1	2	3	4	5	"Agree" (4 and 5) responses	Notes
The workflow tool is easy to use.	0	0	5	50	145	97.5%	Further analysis shows 76% of participants who selected "strongly agree" are tier-one CSRs.
The information available to me when completing a work request is acceptable.	5	40	10	95	50	72.5%	Further analysis shows 95% of the participants who selected "strongly disagree" or "disagree" are tier-two CSRs.
The training provided helped me feel confident about using the workflow tool.	1	2	50	97	50	73.5%	

	1	2	3	4	5	"Agree" (4 and 5) responses	Notes
My ability to complete my work has improved since the workflow tool was implemented.	0	5	55	45	95	70%	Further analysis shows 68% of participants who answered "disagree" or "neutral" are tier-two CSRs.

Reporting

Results from questions about overall satisfaction and dissatisfaction revealed that:

- 97.5 percent of participants find the workflow tool easy to use.
    - 76 percent of the participants who selected "strongly agree" are tier-one customer service representatives. It must be noted that 95.9 percent of tier-one customer service representatives have worked only in an environment with this workflow tool—i.e., they've worked only for XYZ organization and only in departments or on teams that use this workflow tool.
- 72.5 percent of participants think the information available to them when completing a work request is acceptable.
- 73.5 percent of participants find the training provided helpful.
- 70 percent of participants have noticed an improvement in their ability to complete work since the workflow tool was implemented.
    - 68 percent of participants who selected "disagree" or "neutral" within this group are tier-two customer service representatives. Tier-two customer service representatives do not have access to as much information as tier-one customer service representatives.

APPENDIX D Case Study

3. **Please rate how strongly you agree or disagree with the following statements by circling the appropriate number.** The rating scale used was 5=strongly disagree, 4=disagree, 3=neutral, 2=agree, 1=strongly agree.

	1	2	3	4	5	Notes
The process flow takes me through each step in a logical order.	0	0	5	25	170	
The tool moves from one screen to the next screen quickly.	0	50	100	25	25	75% of participants were neutral about the screen-to-screen movement or disagreed that the movement is quick; may want to include improving performance requirements in project scope
Screens are easy to read.	5	10	50	90	45	
Screens are laid out logically for the way I complete my work.	0	0	50	25	125	
I am taken only to screens I need to use within a work request.	0	60	20	55	65	40% of participants were neutral about the screen flow or disagreed that it is effective. May indicate a need to streamline the screen flow for experienced users.

Reporting

Most participants were satisfied with the logical order of the process flow, the readability of screens, and the correlation between screen layout and workflow. However, 75 percent of participants were "neutral" about the screen-to-screen time or disagreed that the transitions were fast; this indicates dissatisfaction with the performance of the tool. The organization may want to consider including improving performance requirements in the scope of the project.

Also, 40 percent of participants were neutral about the screen flow or disagreed that it is effective. This may indicate a need to streamline the screen flow for experienced users.

4. ***In what ways does the current process documentation meet your needs?***
   - It is complete for process flows.
   - Supplemental information helps me answer infrequently asked questions.

In what ways does the current process documentation not meet your needs?
   - There is not enough detail in the process flows.
     - 85 percent of dissatisfied respondents were tier-two CSRs, who do not have access to fully documented process flows.
   - Job aids and supplemental information are often unavailable.
     - 90 percent of dissatisfied respondents were tier-two CSRs. Job aids or supplemental information do not exist for all of their work requests.

5. ***Please rate how strongly you agree or disagree with the following statements by circling the appropriate number.*** The rating scale used was 5=strongly disagree, 4=disagree, 3=neutral, 2=agree, 1=strongly agree.

APPENDIX D Case Study

	1	2	3	4	5	Notes
Process information includes all the detail I need to complete a work request.	25	30	25	50	70	Further analysis shows that 82% of participants who selected "strongly disagree" are team leads; the remaining 18% are tier-two CSRs. 100% of participants who selected "disagree" are tier-two CSRs. This result is reasonable given that tier-two CSRs do not have access to comprehensive process information. Team leads have been trying to address this issue for some time.
Job aids include all the detail I need to complete a work request.	30	25	20	15	110	
Supplementary information includes all the detail I need to complete a work request.	30	25	20	70	55	
The content I need to complete a work request is easy to find.	30	25	50	50	45	

Reporting

- 60 percent of participants are satisfied with the level of detail included in process information; 27.5 percent of participants are dissatisfied.
    - Further analysis shows that 82 percent of participants who selected "strongly disagree" are team leads; the remaining 18 percent

are tier-two CSRs. All participants who selected "disagree" are tier-two CSRs. This result is reasonable given that tier-two CSRs do not have access to comprehensive process information. Team leads have been trying to address this issue for some time.

- The survey found similar levels of satisfaction and dissatisfaction with job aids and supplementary information.

- Satisfaction with the ease of finding content needed to complete a work request was fairly evenly distributed across the rating options.

6. *Please rate how strongly you agree or disagree with the following statements by circling the appropriate number.* The rating scale used was 5=strongly disagree, 4=disagree, 3=neutral, 2=agree, 1=strongly agree.

	1	2	3	4	5	Notes
Training was provided when I needed it.	0	0	50	60	90	75% satisfaction
The trainer explained concepts I did not understand.	0	0	0	100	100	100% satisfaction
I received the right amount of information in training to help me do my job.	5	10	50	85	50	67.5% satisfaction
The approach of the training met my needs as an adult learner.	0	0	60	60	80	70% satisfaction

Reporting

Satisfaction with training was positive.

- 100 percent of participants rated the trainer's competency highly.
- 75 percent stated that training was given at the right time.
- 70 percent felt the training approach was good.
- 67.5 percent felt the amount of training was appropriate.

APPENDIX D Case Study

7. **Please rate how strongly you agree or disagree with the following statements by circling the appropriate number.** The rating scale used was 5=strongly disagree, 4=disagree, 3=neutral, 2=agree, 1=strongly agree.

	1	2	3	4	5	Notes
The workflow tool has improved my day-to-day work.	0	0	50	100	50	Results are consistent with other feedback received in the past.
The workflow tool has increased the professionalism of the customer service representative role.	0	0	100	60	40	

Reporting

Job satisfaction feedback was consistent with other feedback obtained in the past five years.

- 75 percent of participants feel the workflow tool has improved their daily work.

- 50 percent believe the workflow tool has boosted their professionalism.

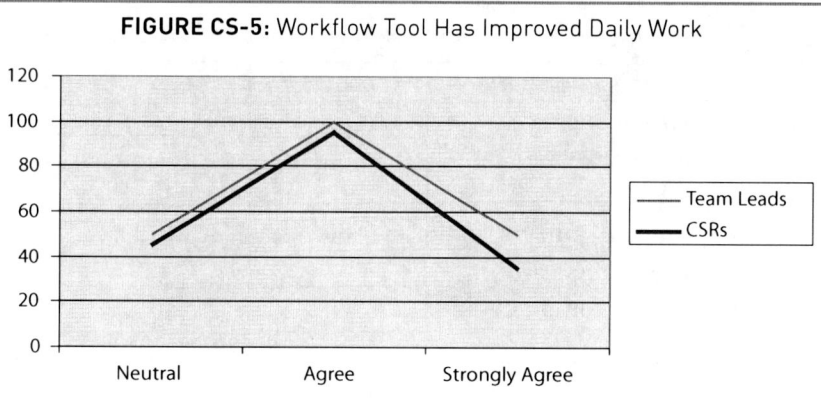

FIGURE CS-5: Workflow Tool Has Improved Daily Work

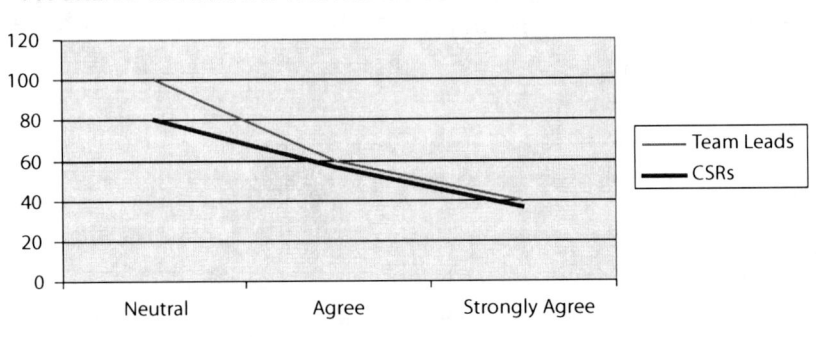

FIGURE CS-6: Workflow Tool Has Increased Professionalism of CSR Role

Results: The Second Objective

1. *Which of the following content improvements would you like to see in the next release? Please select all that apply.*

Option	Number of participants who selected the option	Notes
New types of simple work requests	145	
More supplemental information for simple work requests	55	
Better job aids for simple work requests	100	
Enhanced process information for simple work requests	115	
New types of complex work requests	80	
More supplemental information for complex work requests	80	
Better job aids for complex work requests	80	

Option	Number of participants who selected the option	Notes
Enhanced process information for complex work requests	80	
Other; please specify	35	Responses included: Process information in short form for experienced CSRs More work requests translated into French More work requests translated into Spanish.

Reporting

- "New types of simple work requests" was the option most often selected.

- "Enhanced process information for simple work requests" was the second most frequently selected option.

- "Better job aids for simple work requests" was the third most often selected area for improvement.

- "New types of complex work requests," "more supplemental information for complex work requests," "better job aids for complex work requests," and "enhanced process information for complex work requests" were selected with equal frequency.

- Other desirable options identified by participants were:
    - Condensed process information for experienced customer service representatives
    - More work requests translated into French
    - More work requests translated into Spanish.

Results could also be reported in order of how often each option was selected.

Option	Number of participants who selected the option
New types of simple work requests	145
Enhanced process information for simple work requests	115
Better job aids for simple work requests	100
New types of complex work requests	80
More supplemental information for complex work requests	80
Better job aids for complex work requests	80
Enhanced process information for complex work requests	80
More supplemental information for simple work requests	55

2. *Please rate the importance of each of the following content improvements, where 5=not important, 4=slightly important, 3=average importance, 2= important, and 1=very important.*

	1	2	3	4	5
New types of simple work requests	45	5	0	50	100
More supplemental information for simple work requests	55	0	25	100	20

APPENDIX D Case Study

	1	2	3	4	5
Better job aids for simple work requests	55	0	15	20	110
Enhanced process information for simple work requests	55	0	100	25	20
New types of complex work requests	120	0	5	5	70
More supplemental information for complex work requests	120	0	0	35	45
Better job aids for complex work requests	120	0	0	35	45
Enhanced process information for complex work requests	120	0	0	0	80

Reporting

- New types of simple work requests and better job aids for simple work requests were seen as very important.
- More supplemental information for simple work requests was deemed important.
- New types of complex work requests, more supplemental information for complex work requests, better job aids for complex work requests, and enhanced process information for complex work requests were seen as not important.
  - It must be noted that 60 percent of participants do not work with complex work requests. Options pertaining to complex work requests were rated "very important" by tier-two customer service representatives.

3. *Please rank your top three priorities for content improvements from 1 to 3, with 1 being your top priority.*

	1st	2nd	3rd	Total
New types of simple work requests	100	40	60	200
Enhanced process information for complex work requests	45	65	25	135
New types of complex work requests	20	30	55	105

Better job aids for simple work requests	15	10	0	25
More supplemental information for simple work requests	15	30	0	45
Enhanced process information for simple work requests	5	0	10	15
Better job aids for complex work requests	0	25	40	65
More supplemental information for complex work requests	0	0	10	10
Totals	200	200	200	600

Reporting

The priorities for content improvements are as follows, from highest priority to lowest priority:

- New types of simple work requests
- Enhanced process information for complex work requests
- New types of complex work requests
- Better job aids for complex work requests
- More supplemental information for simple work requests
- Better job aids for simple work requests
- Enhanced process information for simple work requests
- More supplemental information for complex work requests.

Results were compiled by totaling the number of times the option was selected as a first, second, or third priority.

4. *If the background of every screen were changed from black to white, would you be in favor of _____ or against _____ the change?*
   In favor of: 150
   Against: 50

Reporting

Seventy-five percent of participants prefer a white background.

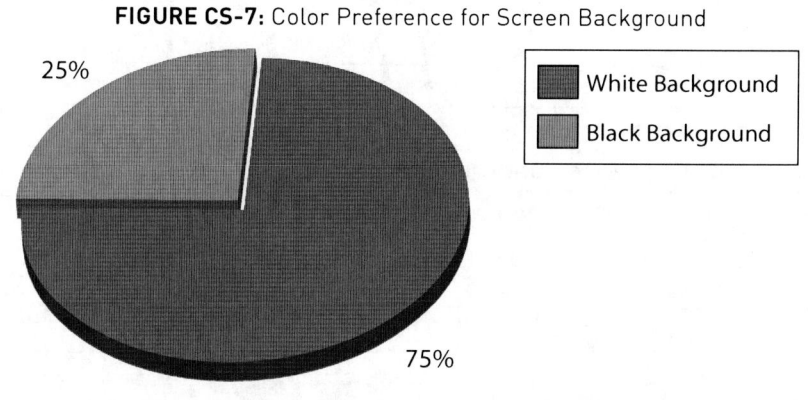

FIGURE CS-7: Color Preference for Screen Background

5. *Which of the following usability improvements would you like to see in the next release?*

Usability improvement	Number of participants who selected the option
Hot key functionality	45
Additional warning messages to prevent errors	185
Streamlined workflow for experienced users	95
Spell checker for user-to-user messages	195
Ability for users to provide online feedback during a work request	15
Ability to change the language of a work request in the workflow	60
Other; please specify	0

Reporting

Usability improvement	Number of participants who selected the option
Spell checker for user-to-user messages	195
Additional warning messages to prevent errors	185
Streamlined workflow for experienced users	95
Ability to change the language of a work request in the workflow	60
Hot key functionality	45
Ability for users to provide online feedback during a work request	15

- No other areas for improvement were identified by participants.
- All bilingual participants selected "ability to change the language of a work request in the workflow."

6. *Please rate the importance of each of the following usability improvements, where 5=not important, 4=slightly important, 3=average importance, 2= important, and 1=very important.*

	1	2	3	4	5
Hot key functionality	10	30	20	100	40
Additional warning messages to prevent errors	5	10	0	85	100
Streamlined workflow for experienced users	30	50	70	10	40
Spell checker for user-to-user messages	1	2	10	87	100
Ability for users to provide online feedback during a work request	100	45	10	30	15
Ability to change the language of a work request in the workflow	50	40	50	10	50

Reporting

- Additional warning messages to prevent errors and spell checker for user-to-user messages were seen as very important.
- Hot key functionality was considered the next most important usability improvement.
- Ability for users to provide online feedback during a work request was deemed not important.

7. *Please rank your top three priorities for usability improvements from 1 to 3, with 1 being your top priority.*

Usability improvement	1st	2nd	3rd	Total
Additional warning messages to prevent errors	95	65	30	190
Spell checker for user-to-user messages	55	45	100	200
Ability to change the language of a work request in the workflow	35	55	0	90
Streamlined workflow for experienced users	15	30	5	50
Hot key functionality	0	5	65	70
Ability for users to provide online feedback during a work request	0	0	0	0
Total	200	200	200	600

Reporting

The priorities for usability improvements are as follows, from highest priority to lowest priority:

- Spell checker for user-to-user messages
- Additional warning messages to prevent errors
- Ability to change the language of a work request in the workflow
- Hot key functionality
- Streamlined workflow for experienced users.

Ability for users to provide online feedback during a work request was never selected as a priority for this release.

Results were compiled by totaling the number of times the option was selected as a first, second, or third priority.

8. *Which of the following new features would you like to see in the next release? Please select all that apply.*

New feature	Number of participants who selected the option
Calculator tools	70
Ability to email customers directly from the tool	175
Ability to import a document and attach it to a work request	160
Ability to combine two work requests into a single work request when appropriate	55
Ability to temporarily stop a work request to answer the phone, then begin a different work request	145
Other; please specify	0

Reporting

New feature	Number of participants who selected the option
Ability to email customers directly from the tool	175
Ability to import a document and attach it to a work request	160
Ability to temporarily stop a work request to answer the phone, then begin a different work request	145

Calculator tools	70
Ability to combine two work requests into a single work request when appropriate	55

No other new features were identified by participants.

9. *Please rate how important each of these possible new features is, where 5=not important, 4=slightly important, 3=average importance, 2= important, and 1=very important.*

	1	2	3	4	5
Calculator tools	15	35	70	35	45
Ability to email customers directly from the tool	0	0	30	65	105
Ability to import a document and attach it to a work request	0	0	25	80	95
Ability to combine two work requests into a single work request when appropriate	45	30	25	60	40
Ability to temporarily stop a work request to answer the phone, then begin a different work request	0	5	10	60	125

Reporting

The ability to temporarily stop a work request to answer the phone, then start a different work request, the ability to email customers directly from the tool, and the ability to import a document and attach it to a work request were seen as very important.

Calculator tools and the ability to combine two work requests into a single work request when appropriate were deemed not important.

10. **Please rank your top three priorities for new features from 1 to 3, with 1 being your top priority.**

	1st	2nd	3rd	Total
Ability to email customers directly from the tool	90	55	60	205
Ability to temporarily stop a work request to answer the phone, then begin a different work request	55	85	65	205
Ability to import a document and attach it to a work request	40	10	0	50
Calculator tools	15	0	0	15
Ability to combine two work requests into a single work request when appropriate	0	50	75	125
Total	200	200	200	600

Reporting

The priorities for new features are as follows, from highest priority to lowest priority:

- Ability to email customers directly from the tool
- Ability to temporarily stop a work request to answer the phone, then begin a different work request
- Ability to combine two work requests into a single work request when appropriate
- Ability to import a document and attach it to a work request
- Calculator tools.

Results were compiled by totaling the number of times the option was selected as a first, second or third priority. The first two features, the ability to email customers and the ability to stop a work request and begin a new one, were considered to be important priorities by equal numbers of participants (205). Just 15 participants thought calculator tools were a top priority.

Only team leads were asked the following three questions.

11. *Which of the following new features would you like to see in the next release?*

Reporting

New feature	Number of participants who selected the option
Reporting on the average amount of time to complete each type of work request, by product	25
Reporting on the average amount of time to complete each type of work request, by customer service representative	25
Real-time data on backlogged queues so that resources can be redirected to work on those queues	25
Daily statistics on work completed by individual customer service representatives	25
Reporting on the range of time to complete each type of work request, by product	10

No other new features were suggested by participants.

12. *Please rate the importance of each of these possible new features, where 5=not important, 4=slightly important, 3=average importance, 2= important, and 1=very important.*

	1	2	3	4	5
Reporting on the average amount of time to complete each type of work request, by product	0	0	0	5	20
Reporting on the average amount of time to complete each type of work request, by customer service representative	0	0	0	0	25

	1	2	3	4	5
Reporting on the range of time to complete each type of work request, by product	2	3	15	3	2
Real-time data on backlogged queues so that resources can be redirected to work on those queues	0	0	0	0	25
Daily statistics on the work completed by individual customer service representatives	0	0	5	15	5

Reporting

- Reporting on the average amount of time to complete each type of work request, by customer service representative; real-time data on backlogged queues so that resources can be redirected to work on those queues; and reporting on the average amount of time to complete each type of work request, by product, were seen as very important.

- Daily statistics on the work completed by individual customer service representatives were seen as important.

- Reporting on the range of time to complete each type of work request, by product, was thought to be of average importance.

13. *Please rank your top three priorities for new features from 1 to 3, with 1 being your top priority.*

	1st	2nd	3rd	Total
Reporting on the average amount of time to complete each type of work request, by customer service representative	15	8	4	27
Real-time data on backlogged queues so that resources can be redirected to work on those queues	8	15	12	35
Daily statistics on the work completed by individual customer service representatives	2	2	9	13

	1st	2nd	3rd	Total
Reporting on the average amount of time to complete each type of work request, by product	0	0	0	0
Reporting on the range of time to complete each type of work request, by product	0	0	0	0
Total	25	25	25	75

Reporting

The priorities for new features for team leaders are as follows, from highest priority to lowest priority:

- Real-time data on backlogged queues so that resources can be redirected to work on those queues
- Reporting on the average amount of time to complete each type of work request, by customer service representative
- Daily statistics on the work completed by individual customer service representatives.

Reporting on the average amount of time to complete each type of work request, by product, and reporting on the range of time to complete each type of work request, by product, were not deemed to be priorities for this release.

Results were compiled by totaling the number of times the option was selected as a first, second, or third priority.

Conclusions

In summary, the survey was seen as successful. Senior management found the information very useful. The team made sure it understood the audience for each report and presented the right amount of information. The team's ability to trace the results of the survey back to its objectives ensured that the stakeholders received the information they had expected.

Glossary

Argument open-ended question — An open-ended question that asks the participant about both sides of an issue.

Closed-ended question — A question that offers a list of response options.

Contributor — Anyone who significantly contributed to the purpose, method, or analysis of a survey and could speak about the survey if asked.

Convenience sample — A sample selected based on the convenience of contacting the participants.

Cover letter — A letter included in every survey that answers the following questions:
- Who is conducting the survey?
- Why is the survey being done?
- What information is being sought?
- How have the participants been selected?
- What will be done with the results?
- Are the answers confidential?
- By when must the survey be completed?
- Will participants get information on the survey results?

Dichotomous item	A form of nominal closed-ended question. Dichotomous items allow the participant to select one of two possible responses.
Frequency distribution	A statistic that identifies the number of times each response appears in the overall data from a question.
Focus group	Administration of a survey in a group setting. Participants can share and discuss their opinions. A trained facilitator conducts the session.
Funneling technique	Beginning a section of a survey with an open-ended question, then moving into closed-ended questions about very specific topics.
Group	Also referred to as a population.
Group-administered survey	Administration of a survey to a group of participants, each of whom completes his or her own survey at the same time. The business analyst supervises and answers questions for clarification.
Incorrect data	Data that do not make sense based on the question asked.
Interval closed-ended question	A closed-ended question with response options that are presented in a logical order. There are equal differences between each adjoining response category for interval closed-ended questions.
Interviewee	A participant in a one-on-one structured interview setting.

Loaded word	A word that can cause a participant to have immediate positive or negative feelings.
Mail-out survey	A survey that is sent to participants. There is no contact between participants and the business analyst. Forms of mail-out surveys include paper mail, email, and online.
Mean	The average of a set of scores.
Meaningless responses	The results from a question that can be answered without any knowledge of the topic.
Median	The point that cuts the distribution of responses in half. The median is sometimes considered the "typical" response.
Missing data	The absence of data if not all participants answer a particular question.
Mode	The most frequently occurring score in a distribution.
Multiple-response item	A form of nominal closed-ended question that allows the participant to select one or more options from a list. Multiple-response items may also be called multiple-choice questions, categorical response items, or checklists.
Nominal closed-ended question	A type of closed-ended question that is generally used to gather factual information. Nominal closed-ended questions are not used to measure amounts.
One-on-one interview	An in-person interview or face-to-face interview.

One-on-one survey	A survey where there is a well-defined list of questions to be asked in each one-on-one survey and a specific order. Questions are not dropped or added from one survey to the next.
Open-ended question	A question that allows participants to answer in their own words. A wide range of responses are possible, and answers are usually longer than one word.
Ordinal closed-ended question	A question that allows the participant to designate the place of an option in an ordered sequence.
Outlying data	Responses that are not consistent with the rest of the data. Also called outliers.
Population	A group of people who have common qualities or characteristics.
Power User	A system user who has the ability to use advanced features of the program that are beyond the abilities of a normal user. A power user is not, however, a programmer and may or may not be a system administrator.
Random sampling	Selecting every nth name from a list of potential participants. Also known as systematic sampling.
Range	The distance between the highest and lowest scores in a distribution.

Ranking-order scale question	A type of ordinal closed-ended question used to gather facts, opinions, attitudes, or judgments. There are equal differences between each adjacent response category for ranking-order scale questions.
Rating-scale question	A question that requires the participant to assign a value to something, but unlike ranking-order scales, the participant is not required to compare one option with other options in the same question.
Recruited sample	A sample composed of participants recruited by phone, email, or in person.
Response rate	The percentage of participants invited to participate in a survey that actually completes the survey.
Sample	The portion of the population included in a survey.
Self-administered survey	Surveying method in which a business analyst meets with participants, but participants fill out the survey by themselves, with or without the business analyst present.
Single-response item	An open-ended question with a blank for the response.
Snowball sample	Sampling technique in which a few participants are contacted and asked to provide referrals to other potential participants.
Skip pattern question	A question that guides the participant to do one of two things based on his or her response.

Stakeholder	A person or group with an interest in the success of a survey.
Stakeholder analysis	A technique used to ensure that all interested parties are identified and their needs, wants, and expectations are understood.
Survey	"A means of eliciting information from many people, anonymously, in a relatively short time" (IIBA® 2006, 177).
Systematic sampling	Selecting every nth name from a list of potential participants. Also called random sampling.
Telephone survey	A survey administered by phone; also known as a telephone poll. A telephone survey should be no more than 15 minutes in length.
Transition	Language used in a survey to show participants that the survey is changing direction.
Unrestricted sampling	Allowing anyone who finds the survey—for example, on the Internet—to participate.

Bibliography

Abbey-Livingston, Diane, and David S. Abbey. *Enjoying Research? A "How-To" Manual on Needs Assessment.* Toronto: Ontario Ministry of Tourism and Recreation, 1982.

Fink, Arlene. *How to Analyze Survey Data.* Thousand Oaks, CA: Sage Publications, 1995.

Fink, Arlene. *How to Report on Surveys.* 2nd ed. Thousand Oaks, CA: Sage Publications, 2003.

Gottesdiener, Ellen. *The Software Requirements Memory Jogger™: A Pocket Guide to Help Software and Business Teams Develop and Manage Requirements.* Salem, NH: GOAL/QPC, 2005.

International Institute of Business Analysis (IIBA®). *A Guide to the Business Analysis Body of Knowledge.* Release 1.6 draft. 2006.

International Institute of Business Analysis, *Survey Techniques in BABOK® v2,* November 7, 2008. For more information, see http://blog.theiiba.org/2008/11/techniques-in-babok-v2.html.

Leffingwell, Dean, and Don Widrig. *Managing Software Requirements: A Unified Approach.* Boston: Addison-Wesley, 2000.

Palys, Ted. *Research Decisions: Quantitative and Qualitative Perspectives.* 2nd ed. Toronto: Harcourt Canada, 1997.

Rathus, Spencer A. *Psychology: Concepts and Connections.* Florence, KY: Thomson Wadworth, 2004.

Spunt, Trevor M. *Guide to Customer Surveys: Sample Questionnaires and Detailed Guidelines for Creating Effective Surveys.* N.p.: The Customer Service Group, 1999.

Thomas, Susan J. *Using Web and Paper Questionnaires for Data-Based Decision Making: From Design to Interpretation of the Results.* Thousand Oaks, CA: Corwin Press, 2004.

Wiegers, Karl E. *More About Software Requirements: Thorny Issues and Practical Advice,* Redmond, WA: Microsoft Press, 2006.

Woodward, Christel A., and Larry W. Chambers. *Guide to Questionnaire Construction and Question Writing.* Hamilton, ON: The Canadian Public Health Association, n.d.

Index

A

acronyms, 45
appearance, of survey, 51–53
appropriate questions, 44
argument open-ended questions, 23–24
attitudes, 20
attributes, 20
audience, 77–78

B

bar charts, 85–86
behavior, 20
behavioral expectation bias, 47
beliefs, 20
bias, 46–48

C

checklist, creating good questions, 44–49
closed-ended questions, 24–25, 70–71
combining questions, 54–56
complex questions, 45

convenience sampling, 16
cover letters
    importance of, 63–66
    pilot surveys, 59–60

D

design elements
    appearance, 51–53
    combining questions, 54–56
    length, 53
    question order, 54
dichotomous items, 25–27
double negatives, 47

F

focus groups, 5
formatting results, 83
frequency distribution, 71–72

G

group-administered surveys, 4
groups, identifying
    importance of, 13
    participants, 15–18
    stakeholders, 13–15

I

incorrect data, 70
International Institute of Business Analysis (IIBA), 1
interval closed-ended questions, 32–37

J

jargon, 45

L

length, of survey, 53
Likert scale item, 41
line charts, 85–86
lists, 83–84
loaded response categories, 48
loaded words, 47

M

mail-out surveys, 4
mean, 72–74
meaningless responses, 48
median, 74
mode, 74–75
multiple-response items, 27–32

N

neutral wording, 46

O

objectives
   determining variables and variations, 8–11
   importance of, 7
   mind map, 10
   setting, 7–8
one-on-one surveys, 5

open-ended questions, 20–23, 70
ordinal closed-ended questions, 37
outlying data, 69–70
oversampling, 16

P

partially closed-ended questions, 27
participants
   convenience sampling, 16
   following up with, 66–67
   oversampling, 15–16
   pilot surveys, 59
   potential, 15
   recruited sampling, 17
   samples, 15–16
   snowball sampling, 16–17
   systematic sampling, 16
   unrestricted sampling, 17
personal questions, 46
pie charts, 84–85
pilot surveys
   analyzing results, 61
   cover letters, 59–60
   importance of, 57
   participants, 59
   process overview, 58–59
   results, 61
prestige bias, 46
process overview, 6

Q

question order, 54
questionnaire. *See* survey
questions
   acronyms, 45
   appropriateness, 44
   argument open-ended, 23–24
   behavioral expectation bias, 47
   bias, 48

INDEX

checklist, 44–49
closed-ended, 24–25
complex, 45
dichotomous items, 25–27
double negatives, 47
importance of, 19
interval closed-ended, 32–37
jargon, 45
Likert scale item, 41
loaded response categories, 48
loaded words, 47
meaningless responses, 48
multiple-response items, 27–32
neutral wording, 46
open-ended, 20–23
ordinal closed-ended, 37
partially closed-ended, 27
personal, 46
precision, 44
prestige bias, 46
rank-order scale item, 37–41
rating scales, 41–44
single-response open-ended, 24
skip pattern, 49
types, 20
vague, 45
wording of, 44

R

random sampling. *See* systematic sampling
range, 76
rank-order scale item, 37–41
rating scales, 41–44
recruited sampling, 17
reports
   audience, 77–78
   bar charts, 85–86
   formatting results, 83
   line charts, 85–86
   lists, 83–84
   pie charts, 84–85
   presentation, 80–83
   tables, 87
   written, 79–80
response rates, 67
results
   closed-ended questions, 70–71
   formatting, 83
   frequency distribution, 71–72
   importance of analyzing, 69–70
   incorrect data, 70
   mean, 72–74
   median, 74
   mode, 74–75
   open-ended questions, 70
   outlying data, 69–70
   pilot surveys, 61
   presenting, 80–83
   range, 76

S

samples, 15–17
self-administered surveys, 4
sending out surveys, 66
single-response open-ended questions, 24
skip pattern, 49
snowball sampling, 16–17
stakeholder analysis chart, 15
stakeholders, 13–15
structured interviews, 4–5
survey
   advantages, 3
   definition, 1
   disadvantages, 3
   history of, 1
   purpose, 1–2
systematic sampling, 16

T
tables, 87
telephone surveys, 5

U
unrestricted sampling, 17

V
vague questions, 45

W
wording, of questions, 44
written reports, 79–80

Complement Your Business Analysis Library with These Additional Resources from
MANAGEMENTCONCEPTS

The Business Analysis Essential Library Series

The *Business Analysis Essential Library* is a series of practical guides that provide insight into the distinct areas of business analysis. This series provides those in the profession with the practical tools and techniques needed to operate effectively. The manuals clarify this emerging role, present contemporary business analysis practices, and explain the practical application of those practices.

*Choose individual volumes... or the complete library...
And use business analysis practices to lead your organization to success!*

Full Set
ISBN 978-1-56726-214-8 ▪ Product Code B148

Professionalizing Business Analysis: Breaking the Cycle of Challenged Projects
Kathleen B. Hass, PMP
ISBN 978-1-56726-208-7 ▪ Product Code B087

Getting It Right: Business Analysis Tools and Techniques
Kathleen B. Hass, PMP, Don J. Wessels, PMP, and Kevin Brennan, PMP
ISBN 978-1-56726-211-7 ▪ Product Code B117

Unearthing Business Requirements: Elicitation Tools and Techniques
Rosemary Hossenlopp, PMP, and Kathleen B. Hass, PMP
ISBN 978-1-56726-210-0 ▪ Product Code B100

The Art and Power of Facilitation: Running Powerful Meetings
Alice Zavala, PMP, and Kathleen B. Hass, PMP
ISBN 978-1-56726-212-4 ▪ Product Code B124

The Business Analyst as Strategist: Translating Business Strategies into Valuable Solutions
Kathleen B. Hass, PMP
ISBN 978-1-56726-209-4 ▪ Product Code B094

From Analyst to Leader: Elevating the Role of the Business Analyst
Kathleen B. Hass, PMP, Richard Vander Horst, PMP, Kimi Ziemski, PMP, and Lori Lindbergh, PMP
ISBN 978-1-56726-213-1 ▪ Product Code B131

MANAGEMENTCONCEPTS

Streamlining Business Requirements: The XCellR8™ Approach
Gerrie Caudle

Many programming systems today are designed and constructed before business requirements are completed and finalized. Without a proper foundation, these systems will eventually crumble. ***Streamlining Business Requirements: The XCellR8™ Approach*** provides business analysts with the foundation, principles, and steps needed to gather and document business requirements in an accurate and efficient manner. Author Gerrie Caudle introduces the XCellR8™ approach, an analysis method used to gather business requirements in a structured, well-defined set of steps.

ISBN 978-1-56726-240-7 ■ Product Code B407, 188 pages

Project Requirements: A Guide to Best Practices
Ralph R. Young

Project Requirements: A Guide to Best Practices gives you tools to improve project success rates, reduce development costs, reduce rework, and accelerate time to market. Based on experience and best practices, this valuable reference will help you improve the management of project requirements, save you time and effort, manage to your schedule, increase customer satisfaction, and drive repeat business. ***Project Requirements: A Guide to Best Practices*** provides project managers with a direct, practical strategy to overcome requirements challenges and manage requirements successfully.

ISBN 978-1-56726-169-1 ■ Product Code B691, 260 pages

How to Save a Failing Project: Chaos to Control
Ralph R. Young, Steven M. Brady, and Dennis C. Nagle, Jr.

Poor project results are all too common and result in dissatisfied customers, users, and project staff. With countless people, goals, objectives, expectations, budgets, schedules, deliverables, and deadlines to consider, it can be difficult to keep projects in focus and on track. ***How to Save a Failing Project: Chaos to Control*** arms project managers with the tools and techniques needed to address these project challenges. The authors provide guidance to develop a project plan, establish a schedule for execution, identify project tracking mechanisms, and implement turn-around methods to avoid failure and regain control.

ISBN 978-1-56726-239-1 ■ Product Code B391, 234 pages

The 77 Deadly Sins of Project Management
Management Concepts

Projects can be negatively impacted by common "sins" that hinder, stall, or throw the project off track. ***The 77 Deadly Sins of Project Management*** helps you better understand how to execute projects by providing individual anecdotes and case studies of the project management sins described by experts in the field.

ISBN 978-1-56726-246-9 ■ Product Code B777, 357 pages

Order today for a 30-day risk-free trial!
Visit **www.managementconcepts.com/pubs** or call **703-790-9595**